Why Has Jesus Not Returned?

Why Has Jesus Not Returned?

The reasons why so many have been mistaken about the return of Jesus Christ

Daniel Botha

ROCKWALL PUBLISHING

Copyright ©2008 Daniel Botha
All rights reserved. No part of this publication may be reproduced, stored in a retrieval system or transmitted in any form or by any means, electronic, mechanical, photocopying, recording or otherwise, without the prior written permission of the publisher.

ISBN 10:   0-9799385-0-3
ISBN 13:   978-0-9799385-0-4

Published by Rockwall Publishing, P O Box 2288, Rockwall TX, 75087
Design and layout by SelfPblishing.com
Printed in the United States of America

This is a **RockwallPublishing**.com book.

Contents

Which Bible to Use vii
Dedication ix
Preface xi

Will Jesus Return? 1
Millennium Madness 9
The Seven-Thousand-Year Plan of God 15
What about the Signs of His Coming? 19
The Signs of the Times 29
Religious Persecution 33
The Great Falling Away 37
The Sign of the End 43
The Abomination of Desolation 59
The Great Tribulation 69
How Will Jesus Return? 77
The Parable of the Fig Tree 85
No One Knows the Day or the Hour 89
My Lord Delayeth His Coming 97
The Parable of the Ten Virgins 101
The Parable of the Talents 107
What Have We Learned? 113
Conclusion 115
Epilogue 119

Which Bible to Use

QUOTES FROM the Bible in this book are primarily drawn from the King James Version (KJV), arguably the translation most widely distributed—and the easiest and most affordable to acquire—as well as one of the most accurate. Occasionally, I refer to the New International Version (NIV), where it more readily clarifies a discussion. Assume, however, that I have used the KJV, unless otherwise noted in the text. Note that where the KJV translators have inserted words for ease of reading that do not appear in the original Hebrew or Greek, they have generally placed them in italics. This enables one to see exactly what the original texts say.

For ease of reference, I include the full quotation of virtually every passage of scripture I refer to. My earnest desire is for you to read the scriptures in full and believe them. When referencing passages in your own Bible to glean the context, as I hope you will do, I would suggest that you use an actual translation, not a paraphrase. While a paraphrase of the Bible may be easy to read, it is not as accurate as a translation and must be used with caution.

For the same ease of reading, I have placed scriptural references at the beginning of highlighted quotations rather than at the end so you would know immediately where we are reading from, like one does when giving, or listening to, a sermon.

Dedication

TO MY wife Helen who, for over forty years, has labored faithfully by my side, serving the people of God.

To my children—Lois, David, and Jonathan—who so patiently endured endless hours of their dad's preaching.

And to my many friends who encouraged me to keep writing, and to my editors and publishers, who have made my dreams to publish books come true.

Preface

I HAVE WAITED for the return of Jesus for a long time. In 1955, when still a teenager, I heard a sermon during which the preacher told us, "Jesus could come tonight! There have been wars, famines, pestilence, and earthquakes in diverse places. You must repent because Jesus could come tonight." I remember how much that sermon scared me. It seemed like all the end-time events were taking place and the return of Jesus was imminent, right at the door.

Of course, Jesus did not come in 1955, nor did he come in the '60s, '70s, '80s, or '90s. Nor did he come at the end of the second millennium, when some expected him to return. Why not? Were all the preachers who preached about the return of Jesus mistaken?

Jesus said, "Watch therefore, for ye know neither the day nor the hour wherein the Son of man cometh" (Matthew 25:13). Why then have so many Christians thought that Jesus was going to come at a certain time? How could so many sincere people have been so sadly mistaken? There have been times when some Christians have sold their possessions and gathered together, waiting for Jesus to return, only to be deeply disappointed.

Now we are in the twenty-first century, and life seems to be continuing as it always has. For some, life is much better. In the developed world, we live longer, have more, and live in relative peace. For many, it is quite a nice life. However, many people are not that fortunate. Famine, pestilence, and wars still exist. Terrorism has brought the specter of war and death close to many, if not all, of us, but most of us are just busy with our daily activities. We work, our children go to school, we plan our vacations, and we do not worry too much about the return of Jesus. That idea seems to have disappeared from many people's thinking.

Does the Bible really say Jesus is coming back? Or is that just an idea from a bygone era when people were in error, when preachers were just deluded? Have we now come to realize that Jesus is not coming? For so long people have waited, in vain it seems, for Jesus to return. What does the Bible really say about Jesus' return, and, more importantly, what did Jesus say about his return?

Through the centuries, so many sincere people have been certain that Jesus would return in their lifetimes. But they died without seeing the return of Jesus. Why were they wrong?

Today, some still talk about Jesus' return. Many preachers still say, "Jesus could come very soon." They say, "Look at what is happening in the world. Look at the wars, the famine, and the disease epidemics. Look at the threat of the HIV/AIDS pandemic. Millions are going to die, and Jesus is going to return soon!" Will he really come tomorrow, or next year, or the year after that? Or are today's preachers just as mistaken as the preachers in the past were?

The people of the Middle Ages endured wars. There was the Black Death that killed an estimated seventy-five million worldwide. Times were terrible. But Jesus did not return. After that there came great religious wars. Then, in the twentieth century, came World War I, the "war to end all wars." It was followed by the 1918 world flu pandemic that killed millions. Those were grim days, and people talked about the "time of the end." But it was not the "time of the end," nor was World War II. In fact, the generation of World War II is now dying and Jesus still has not returned. What next?

What did Jesus of Nazareth really say about the time of his Second Coming? What is it that preachers, through the ages, have not understood? We need to find out. We need to uncover what Jesus said about his return so we can clearly answer the question: why has Jesus not returned?

Will Jesus Return?

MOST CHRISTIANS are familiar with the story of the birth, life, death, burial, and resurrection of Jesus. Some may even be able to turn to some of the scriptures that mention these events, scriptures like:

> **Luke 2:11–12** For unto you is born this day in the city of David a Saviour, which is Christ the Lord. And this *shall be* a sign unto you; ye shall find the babe wrapped in swaddling clothes, lying in a manger.

> **Luke 2:39–40** And when they had performed all things according to the law of the Lord, they returned into Galilee, to their own city Nazareth. And the child grew, and waxed strong in spirit, filled with wisdom: and the grace of God was upon him.

> **Matthew 20:18–19** Behold, we go up to Jerusalem; and the Son of man shall be betrayed unto the chief priests and unto the scribes, and they shall condemn him to death, and shall deliver him to the Gentiles to mock, and to scourge, and to crucify *him*: and the third day he shall rise again.

> **Matthew 27:57–60** When the even was come, there came a

rich man of Arimathaea, named Joseph, who also himself was Jesus' disciple: He went to Pilate, and begged the body of Jesus. Then Pilate commanded the body to be delivered. And when Joseph had taken the body, he wrapped it in a clean linen cloth, and laid it in his own new tomb, which he had hewn out in the rock: and he rolled a great stone to the door of the sepulchre, and departed.

Matthew 28:5–7 And the angel answered and said unto the women, Fear not ye: for I know that ye seek Jesus, which was crucified. He is not here: for he is risen, as he said. Come, see the place where the Lord lay. And go quickly, and tell his disciples that he is risen from the dead; and, behold, he goeth before you into Galilee; there shall ye see him: lo, I have told you.

The scriptures about the birth, life, death, burial, and resurrection of Jesus seem so clear. And the scriptures about his return are just as clear:

Acts 1:9–11 And when he [Jesus] had spoken these things, while they beheld, he was taken up; and a cloud received him out of their sight. And while they looked stedfastly toward heaven as he went up, behold, two men stood by them in white apparel; which also said, Ye men of Galilee, why stand ye gazing up into heaven? This same Jesus, which is taken up from you into heaven, shall so come in like manner as ye have seen him go into heaven.

Matthew 24:27 For as the lightning cometh out of the east, and shineth even unto the west; so shall also the coming of the Son of man be.

Luke 21:27 And then shall they see the Son of man coming in a cloud with power and great glory.

These are just a few scriptures in which we can read about Jesus' return. It seems so clear that he will return. Why then the confusion about *when* he will return? Some are quick to point out that Jesus said, "But of that day and hour knoweth no *man*, no, not the angels of heaven, but my Father only" (Matthew 24:36). That is true. Jesus did say that. Why then have so many preachers told us that we are living in the end times or that Jesus may come soon? Preachers have been saying that for centuries, and many are still saying it. Why?

Amazingly, even in New Testament times, some thought the kingdom would immediately appear:

Luke 19:11 And as they heard these things, he [Jesus] added and spake a parable, because he was nigh to Jerusalem, and because they thought that the kingdom of God should immediately appear.

While Jesus was still on Earth, even before his crucifixion, some thought that he was going to set up the Kingdom of God—at that time! How did Jesus correct their thinking?

Luke 19:12 He said therefore, a certain nobleman went into a far country to receive for himself a kingdom, and to return.

Jesus was the nobleman who had to go to a far country to receive the Kingdom. The far country was heaven. Jesus knew he had to be crucified, buried, and resurrected, and ascend to heaven. Only then would he return. That should have been clear to everyone who heard Jesus speak this parable—the nobleman had to go to a far country, to heaven, then to return. But the question still remained: *when* would he return? Even Jesus' own disciples wondered about this. After Jesus had died and been resurrected, he appeared to his disciples:

> **Acts 1:3** To whom also he shewed himself alive after his passion by many infallible proofs, being seen of them forty days, and speaking of the things pertaining to the kingdom of God:

Jesus had spent three-and-a-half years teaching his disciples. Then they saw him crucified. Some of them went to the empty tomb. Then they saw the resurrected Jesus. Now he had spent forty days with them. Notice the question they asked Jesus:

> **Acts 1:6** When they therefore were come together, they asked of him, saying, Lord, wilt thou at this time restore again the kingdom to Israel?

After all of Jesus' teaching, the disciples still wondered whether the Kingdom would appear soon. Notice Jesus' answer:

> **Acts 1:7** And he said unto them, It is not for you to know the times or the seasons, which the Father hath put in his own power.

It sounds like the same old story people give you when you ask about the return of Jesus—"It is not for you to know the times or the seasons." Why then should we even bother to think about the return of Jesus? Is it really important? Should we not just live our lives as Christians and not worry about *when* Jesus will return?

Long before his death and resurrection, Jesus told his disciples, "After this manner therefore pray ye: Our Father which art in heaven, Hallowed be thy name. Thy kingdom come. Thy will be done in earth, as it is in heaven" (Matthew 6:9–10). Jesus told his disciples, and now tells all of us, through his words recorded for us in the New Testament, to pray, "Thy kingdom come." What does this mean? Does it mean the Kingdom will come in our hearts? Does it mean the church is the Kingdom? If so, there is no need for Jesus to return. But, if it means that Jesus will come as "KING OF KINGS, AND LORD OF LORDS" (Revelation 19:16), then it is very important that we should pray for it, and look forward to it.

The apostle Paul certainly looked forward to the return of Jesus. He wrote to Timothy, his friend and fellow minister:

> **1 Timothy 6:13–16** I give thee charge in the sight of God, who quickeneth all things, and before Christ Jesus, who before Pontius Pilate witnessed a good confession; That thou keep this commandment without spot, unrebukeable, until the appearing of our Lord Jesus Christ: Which in his times he shall shew, who is the blessed and only Potentate, the King of kings, and Lord of lords; Who only hath immortality, dwelling in the light which no man can approach unto; whom no man hath seen, nor can see: to whom be honour and power everlasting. Amen.

Paul knew that Jesus was going to appear as "King of kings and Lord of lords." Paul wrote these words years before John wrote them in the book of Revelation: "And he hath on *his* vesture and on his thigh a name written, KING OF KINGS, AND LORD OF LORDS" (Revelation 19:16). Paul eagerly looked forward to the return of Jesus as King of kings and Lord of lords. He also wrote to the church in Thessalonica:

> **1 Thessalonians 4:16–17** For the Lord himself shall descend from heaven with a shout, with the voice of the archangel, and with the trump of God: and the dead in Christ shall rise first: Then we which are alive *and* remain shall be caught up together with them in the clouds, to meet the Lord in the air: and so shall we ever be with the Lord.

According to these verses, Paul looked forward to the return of Jesus because that would be when "the dead in Christ"—those who died having truly accepted Christ, and become his disciples—would rise.

Why, we may ask, do the dead need to rise? Why does there need to be a resurrection? Surely, if the righteous dead have gone to heaven, as many believe they do, why then should the dead in Christ rise? Why should the trumpet blow and the resurrection occur? Or is it just too embarrassing to ask such awkward questions? Jesus said, "And ye shall know the truth, and the truth shall make you free" (John 8:32). What is the truth that will set us free from confusion and doubt?

Were the disciples mistaken in thinking that Jesus was going to return as King of kings? Of course not! However, they did think Jesus would return soon. Read again what Paul wrote in 1 Thessalonians 4:17, "We which are alive *and* remain shall be caught up together with them in the clouds, to meet the Lord in the air." When Paul wrote these words, he thought the return of Jesus would happen *in his lifetime*. He wrote similar words to the Corinthians:

> **1 Corinthians 15:51–52** Behold, I shew you a mystery; we shall not all sleep, but we shall all be changed, in a moment, in the twinkling of an eye, at the last trump: for the trumpet shall sound, and the dead shall be raised incorruptible, and we shall be changed.

The trumpet would sound, Paul wrote, and the dead would be raised, and *we*—all Christians, including Paul—would be changed. There is no question that, at the time he wrote this, Paul thought he would see the return of Jesus in his lifetime. But it did not happen. Later in his life, when Paul was a prisoner in Rome, he wrote to Timothy:

> **2 Timothy 4:7–8** I have fought a good fight, I have finished *my* course, I have kept the faith: Henceforth there is laid up for me a crown of righteousness, which the Lord, the righteous judge, shall give me at that day: and not to me only, but unto all them also that love his appearing.

By the time he wrote this second letter to Timothy, Paul knew he would die before Jesus returned. But Paul still looked forward to the day of Jesus' return because that would be the time when Jesus would give him his "crown of righteousness."

Why has there been so much confusion over when Jesus will

return? Because Jesus never gave us an exact date! That is clear. But, there also has been some deliberate deception regarding the return of Jesus. Jesus predicted this, as we will see. There also is no question that many were just mistaken. Many Christians, through the ages, thought Jesus would come *soon*, but he did not. We need to look at some of the mistakes they made in thinking that Jesus would return in their lifetimes and make sure we avoid those same mistakes.

First, why is it that some Christians thought that Jesus was going to come at the end of the millennium? As the clock struck midnight on December 31, 1999, and celebrations began, many of us were glued to our television sets watching marvelous fireworks displays, starting in New Zealand and continuing in Australia, England, and many other countries. Many people stayed up all night to see the spectacular displays—so did some Christians who were convinced that Jesus would now return. Of course, there were some who said the old millennium did not end till December 31, *2000*. When that day came, there were also a few who were out "waiting for the Lord."

But Jesus did not come at the end of 1999, nor at the end of 2000. It is now time to analyze some of the basic mistakes people have made in thinking that Jesus would soon come.

Millennium Madness

WHEN WE approached the year AD 2000, some really thought Jesus would return. Why? We need to understand why such thinking was wrong.

When we look at history, we find that the same thing occurred in AD 1000, at the end of the first millennium after Christ. Some sold their goods, gathered together, and waited for Jesus to return. Why? Because it was the end of the "millennium."

What is a "millennium"? It comes from the Latin *mille* (thousand) and *annus* (year)—a thousand years. When the first millennium ended, some thought Jesus would come. When the second millennium came, far more people thought he would come. In fact, there still are preachers that are claiming that Jesus will come back soon because the millennium has just ended.

Does the millennium really have anything to do with the return of Jesus? Let us understand. The date we have is based on a calendar that was implemented by the Roman emperor Julius Caesar, who lived just before the time of Jesus. It was during the reign of his son, Augustus Caesar, that Jesus was born, "And it came to pass in those days, that there went out a decree from Caesar Augustus, that all the world should be taxed" (Luke 2:1). The world Rome ruled over included all territories around the Mediterranean. It included Galilee and Judea, the areas in Palestine where many Jews lived. Every person in the empire had to go to his or her city for a census, and to be taxed. That is why Joseph had to take his nine-month-pregnant wife, Mary, all the way from Nazareth in Galilee where they were living, to Bethlehem, the city of David, where the descendants of David had come from. God had inspired the emperor of the Roman Empire, one of the most powerful men on the earth at that time, to make a decision that would cause the prophecy to be fulfilled that Jesus would be born in Bethlehem, the city of David.

In 1582, Pope Gregory XIII changed the calendar that Julius Caesar's scholars designed after it was found that the calendar was not accurate enough. We now have what is known as the Gregorian calendar. This is the calendar that is today generally accepted worldwide, even though some still refer to other calendars, especially in the practice of religions.

When the end of the second millennium came, had it really been two thousand years since the birth of Jesus? Surprisingly, no! Jesus was actually born before 4 BC (BC stands for "before Christ"), or, as some prefer, 4 BCE ("before the common era") to be politically correct. AD stands for *anno Domini*, Latin for "in the year of our Lord."

How do we know Jesus was born before 4 BC? How could Jesus Christ have been born "before Christ"? That does sound strange. Let us understand:

Matthew 2:1–2 Now when Jesus was born in Bethlehem of Judaea in the days of Herod the king, behold, there came wise men from the east to Jerusalem, saying, Where is he that is born King of the Jews? for we have seen his star in the east, and are come to worship him.

The wise men came from the east to see Jesus. It was during the time of Herod the Great:

> **Matthew 2:13** And when they [the wise men, after their visit to the child] were departed, behold, the angel of the Lord appeareth to Joseph in a dream, saying, Arise, and take the young child and his mother, and flee into Egypt, and be thou there until I bring thee word: for Herod will seek the young child to destroy him.

Joseph, Mary, and Jesus fled to Egypt where they stayed "until the death of Herod" (Matthew 2:15). History is clear that Herod the Great died in 4 BC. Jesus was born before Herod died, so he must have been born before 4 BC.

What does this have to do with millennia? The answer is simple. The dates AD 1000 and AD 2000 are just dates, man-made numbers with no exact significance in and of themselves. Preachers using these dates to scare people into doing something rash because of Jesus' supposed return was just plain ignorant, or worse, deceptive. They ought to have known better.

In Uganda, in central Africa, Joseph Kibwetere, an infamous African cult leader, led a cult called the "Movement for the Restoration of the Ten Commandments of God." In 2001, this cult ended with a horrific mass murder/suicide that claimed the lives of hundreds of followers. This tragedy occurred after doomsday predictions made by Kibwetere and his accomplice, Credonia Mwerinde, failed to materialize at the turn of the millennium.

What happened in Uganda reminded me of the "Jonestown Massacre," in November 1978, when 913—including 408 Americans—of the 1100 members of Jim Jones' People's Temple died in a mass suicide. The cult, started in California, had moved to Guyana in 1974, apparently in anticipation of the Lord's return.

There was also the suicide of the thirty-eight members of the Heaven's Gate cult who were found dead in a rented mansion in the upscale San Diego community of Rancho Santa Fe, California, on March 26, 1997. They apparently believed Jesus was on a spaceship that was hiding behind the Hale-Bop Comet that appeared at that time.

As we shall see, Jesus warned against this type of tragic deception. Unfortunately, there has been, and will be, far more deception than what occurred in these isolated incidences.

But, some may ask, doesn't the Bible talk about a millennium—a thousand years? Most certainly! Let us read it:

Revelation 20:4 and they lived and reigned with Christ a thousand years.

According to this verse, the saints will live and reign with Jesus for a thousand years. We can look at other verses that tie in with this one:

Revelation 2:26 And he that overcometh, and keepeth my works unto the end, to him will I give power over the nations:

Revelation 5:10 And hast made us unto our God kings and priests: and we shall reign on the earth.

Will Jesus really come and reign over the nations on this earth with the resurrected saints for a thousand years? Yes, Revelation does say that, but does it say he will come at the end of a millennium? No, it does not.

Some have referred to another scripture that mentions a thousand years, a scripture written by the apostle Peter:

> **2 Peter 3:8** But, beloved, be not ignorant of this one thing, that one day *is* with the Lord as a thousand years, and a thousand years as one day.

Why did Peter write this? Did he know that the return of Jesus was still two thousand years away? No! Let us read what he wrote and why he wrote it. To understand the context of any scripture, one should always read the preceding verses:

> **2 Peter 3:3–7** Knowing this first, that there shall come in the last days scoffers, walking after their own lusts, and saying, Where is the promise of his coming? for since the fathers fell asleep, all things continue as *they were* from the beginning of the creation. For this they willingly are ignorant of, that by the word of God the heavens were of old, and the earth standing out of the water and in the water: Whereby the world that then was, being overflowed with water, perished: But the heavens and the earth, which are now, by the same word are kept in store, reserved unto fire against the day of judgment and perdition of ungodly men.

Even in Peter's day, some were scoffing at the idea that Jesus was going to return. Peter reminded them that, in the days of Noah, there were also scoffers who then died in the flood. In the same way, those who scoff at the idea of the return of Jesus will die in fire. Peter wrote that there is going to come a "day of judgment and perdition of ungodly men" (2 Peter 3:7).

Was Peter giving us a formula to calculate when Jesus is going to return by saying, "One day *is* with the Lord as a thousand years, and a thousand years as one day" (2 Peter 3:8)? If Peter did, he could have written, "Jesus is not going to come for another two thousand years." Peter never wrote that. The reason Peter wrote what he did was to warn people not to scoff at the idea of Jesus' return. According to the word of God, Jesus is going to return, but it will be in God's time, not ours. Peter continued:

> **2 Peter 3:9** The Lord is not slack concerning his promise, as some men count slackness; but is longsuffering to us-ward, not willing that any should perish, but that all should come to repentance.

Peter said God is patient and he is giving us time to repent. But that time will run out, just as it did for the people in Noah's day. Peter was giving a warning to scoffers. Peter was *not* giving a formula to work out when Jesus was going to return.

Is there a scriptural reason we should have thought that Jesus would come at the end of the millennium? No! The Bible never says that Jesus will come at the end of a millennium, and the dates, AD 1000 and AD 2000, are man's dates written on a calendar. They have no spiritual significance as such.

The Seven-Thousand-Year Plan of God

ANOTHER IDEA that contributed to the belief that Jesus would return at the end of the second millennium is "the seven-thousand-year plan of God." What is this, and where did the idea come from?

We read in:

Genesis 2:1–3 Thus the heavens and the earth were finished, and all the host of them. And on the seventh day God ended his work which he had made; and he rested on the seventh day from all his work which he had made. And God blessed the seventh day, and sanctified it: because that in it he had rested from all his work which God created and made.

God, according to Genesis, created the earth in six days; then he rested. Israel was reminded of this in the fourth commandment, given at Mt. Sinai:

Exodus 20:8–11 Remember the sabbath day, to keep it holy. Six days shalt thou labour, and do all thy work: But the seventh day *is* the sabbath of the LORD thy God: *in it* thou shalt not do any work, thou, nor thy son, nor thy daughter, thy manservant, nor thy maidservant, nor thy cattle, nor thy stranger that *is* within thy gates: For *in* six days the LORD made heaven and earth, the sea, and all that in them *is*, and rested the seventh day: wherefore the LORD blessed the sabbath day, and hallowed it.

The seven-thousand-year plan of God is based on the idea that because God gave man six days in which to work, followed by the Sabbath, so God has given mankind six thousand years to continue in the footsteps of Adam and Eve, deciding for themselves what is good or evil, enduring all the painful lessons of experience—every man doing that which is right in his own eyes—followed by one thousand years of *rest* after Jesus returns.

Is there a future *rest* promised to Christians? We read:

Hebrews 4:1 Let us therefore fear, lest, a promise being left *us* of entering into his rest, any of you should seem to come short of it.

The book of Hebrews draws a parallel between the journey of the nation of Israel to the Promised Land and our Christian journey. Under Joshua, Israel entered the Promised Land, but they did not find rest; they found war after war, vividly depicted in the book of Judges.

Hebrews continues:

Hebrews 4:8–11 For if Jesus [Joshua] had given them rest, then would he not afterward have spoken of another day. There remaineth therefore a rest to the people of God. For he that is entered into his rest, he also hath ceased from his own works, as God *did* from his. Let us labour therefore to enter into that rest, lest any man fall after the same example of unbelief.

The book of Hebrews is clear: Israel did not enter a period of rest, but there will be a rest for the people of God—a future Sabbath rest. That rest is equated with the one-thousand-year rule of Jesus and the saints as mentioned in Revelation 20:4. Under the rule of Jesus and his saints this world will be at peace.

But, are these verses giving us a formula to determine when Jesus will return? Not at all! The problem with trying to calculate when Jesus will return, using the seven-thousand-year plan, is that it is impossible to figure out exactly how long it has been since God created Adam. All we know, using Biblical history and chronology, is that there were *about* four thousand years from Adam to the birth of Jesus, and there have been *about* two thousand years since Jesus' birth. We can refer to other calendars, such as the Jewish, Tamil, and others and find that, theoretically, we are living in the sixth millennium. The Bible does tell us that there is a future rest for the people of God. Jesus, according to Revelation 20:4, will rule the earth with his saints for a thousand years. But when that thousand years will begin, we cannot calculate.

So, to have used the seven-thousand-year plan of God to determine when Jesus would return was, and is, a mistake, yet many are still trying to calculate when the return of Jesus will be. Any dates they may come up with are just that, *dates*, with no real significance.

What about the Signs of His Coming?

JUST BEFORE the end of the millennium, a friend of mine in Texas said to me, "We have sold our house; we are giving all the money to our church because Jesus is coming back."

I asked her, "How do you know Jesus is coming back?"

She said, "Look at all the earthquakes we have been having, and the famines, and diseases. What about the AIDS epidemic? Are not all these signs of his coming?"

It came as a surprise to her, and it may surprise you, but my answer to her was, "No, these are *not* the signs of the imminent return of Jesus! Wars, famines, pestilence, and earthquakes are not signs of the imminent return of Jesus."

Someone coined the phrase, "What would Jesus do?" And many Christians walk around with badges and jewelry with the initials "WWJD?" to help them remember to act the way Jesus acted. I have encouraged people to ask, "What did Jesus *say*?" This is so important. What *did* Jesus say? Do we really know what Jesus said about his return? What did he say about the signs of his coming?

Let's refer to the one prophecy in which Jesus talked about the events that would precede his coming. It is called the Olivet Prophecy because Jesus was sitting on the Mount of Olives, east of Jerusalem, when he spoke this prophecy to his disciples. It is found in Matthew 24, Mark 13, and Luke 21. Here, we can see exactly what Jesus said about his return. Even if you have read the Bible for many years, be prepared for some surprises.

Let us slowly and carefully read what Jesus said, starting with Matthew's account:

> **Matthew 24:1** And Jesus went out, and departed from the temple: and his disciples came to *him* for to shew him the buildings of the temple.

Jesus and his disciples were walking past the temple and its buildings. For those who do not know much about the temple that stood in Jerusalem, let's review.

In about 900 BC, King Solomon built the first temple for God on that site (1 Kings 6). About three hundred years later, the Babylonian armies destroyed that temple: "And they burnt the house of God, and brake down the wall of Jerusalem, and burnt all the palaces thereof with fire, and destroyed all the goodly vessels thereof" (2 Chronicles 36:19). The Jews were taken into captivity to Babylon. After seventy years, at the time of Ezra and Nehemiah, 42,360 Jews returned to Jerusalem to rebuild the city and the temple (Ezra 1:64). Most of the Jews stayed in the Diaspora, the scattering. After more than four hundred years, this "second temple," as it was called, was in need of restoration. Before the birth of Jesus, Herod the Great started a vast building project to restore the temple for the Jews. After Herod's death, his son, Herod Antipas, continued the work. The Jews were very excited about this restoration. Some were even called "Herodians" (Matthew 22:16; Mark 3:6, 12:13) because they thought Herod was sent by God to rebuild the temple. The disciples had pointed out this building project to Jesus. Instead of marveling at it, we read:

> **Matthew 24:2** And Jesus said unto them, See ye not all these things? Verily I say unto you, there shall not be left here one stone upon another, that shall not be thrown down.

Jesus told his disciples that this temple would also be destroyed. From the area of the temple, Jesus and his disciples would have walked down through the Valley of Kidron, then up the Mount of Olives. We can only imagine what the disciples were thinking as they walked along with Jesus. They had shown Jesus the temple buildings, and he said they would all be torn down. Then they sat down on the Mount of Olives. Below them was the city, with the temple standing prominently.

It must have been interesting for the disciples to sit with Jesus on the Mount of Olives knowing full well that the prophet Zechariah wrote, "And his feet shall stand in that day [of the Lord's return] upon the mount of Olives" (Zechariah 14:4). It was inevitable that the disciples would ask the next question:

> **Matthew 24:3** And as he sat upon the mount of Olives, the disciples came unto him privately, saying, Tell us, when shall these things be? and what *shall be* the sign of thy coming, and of the end of the world?

Jesus had told them that not one stone of the temple would be left on another, that Jerusalem and the temple would again be destroyed. When you stand on the Mount of Olives, you have a panoramic view of all of Jerusalem. That is what Jesus and the disciples were looking at, and Jesus said Jerusalem and the temple would be destroyed. Then the disciples asked, "when shall these things be?"—when the temple would be destroyed. (About forty years later, the Roman army, under

Titus, would come from the north and destroy the temple.) But the disciples also asked, "And what shall be the sign of thy coming, and of the end of the world?" That is the same question Christians have asked over the past two thousand years—what shall be the sign of Jesus' coming and of the end of the world? How did Jesus answer the question? Be prepared to be surprised:

Matthew 24:4 And Jesus answered and said unto them, Take heed that no man deceive you.

The first thing Jesus said, when the disciples asked him about his return, was that they should take heed that they would not be deceived. How amazing. Would some really try to deceive the disciples of Jesus about Jesus' return? Yes! That is what Jesus said. How can we make sure that we are not deceived about Jesus' return? By finding out exactly what Jesus said.

Have I been deceived? Have you been deceived? Surely not, we might say. But Jesus told his disciples, "Take heed that no man deceive you." These words of Jesus were recorded for us. How amazing this should be to us. Chances are you have heard preachers say, "Watch the Middle-east!" or "Watch Iraq or Iran." In the days of the Cold War, some said, "Watch the Soviet Union." Talk to anyone about the prophecies of the end-time, and they will tell you to "Watch!" They will give you something to watch. "Watch the Muslims," has now become a popular warning following the September 11, 2001, terrorist attacks on the United States. Yes, preachers tell us to watch what is happening in the world, but Jesus said, "Watch out that no one deceives you" (Matthew 24:4 NIV). How would some try to deceive the disciples of Jesus?

Jesus continued:

Matthew 24:5 For many shall come in my name, saying, I am Christ; and shall deceive many.

Jesus said, "For many shall come in my name." How many people come "in Jesus' name"? Many! Today, there are an estimated two billion Christians on Earth. There are thousands upon thousands of Christian churches. How many Christians or Christian preachers stand up and speak "in Jesus' name"? Many!

Where you live, there may be several Christian churches. You may know several good Christian people who help their neighbors and follow Jesus' instruction, "Thou shalt love thy neighbour as thyself" (Matthew 22:39). I have known many. Their selfless dedication to help others has always astounded me. There are Christians who feed the poor, visit the sick and those in prison. There are Christians who comfort the grieving, and nurture the destitute. It is so wonderful to see people who come "in Jesus' name" and do good.

But Jesus said, many—not a few—many, would come in his name and deceive. Are there really many who would use the name of Jesus to deceive? Is that possible? Yes, that is what Jesus said. Try to think back over the past two thousand years of Christianity. Think of what was done in the name of Jesus:

- In the name of Jesus, people have been persecuted!
- In the name of Jesus, people have been killed!
- In the name of Jesus, racism has been preached and practiced!
- In the name of Jesus, wars have been fought!

The list is endless. So many horrific things have been done in

Jesus' name. If you know the history of Christianity, you know that there were times when some churches actually fought against each other, Christians killing Christians. Not all Christianity has been true Christianity.

Turn on the TV, and watch several evangelists. Each claims to have the truth of God. But do they all agree? Of course not! How then can we know what true Christianity is? We need to go back to the one after whom Christianity is named, Jesus Christ.

But Jesus also said they will say, "I am Christ." How many have come to you and said that they were Jesus Christ? In over forty years of being a Christian, this has never happened to me. I once met a man in the KwaZulu-Natal province of South Africa who claimed to be Melchizedek (Genesis 14 & Hebrews 7). Of course, this man was deluded. I met a man on the island of Mauritius who claimed to be Michael the archangel. He also was deluded and certainly was no angel. I met two men in Pretoria, a city in the Gauteng province of South Africa, who claimed to be the "two witnesses" of Revelation 11. They were not. Yes, I have met a few interesting, but rather odd, people, but I have never met anyone who claimed to be Jesus Christ. Chances are neither have you.

But Jesus said, "For many shall come in my name, saying, I am Christ." Was Jesus mistaken when he said this? Of course not! Later, in this same chapter, Jesus said, "For there shall arise false Christs, and false prophets, and shall shew great signs and wonders; insomuch that, if *it were* possible, they shall deceive the very elect" (Matthew 24:24). Yes, Jesus said there will come a time when there will be false Christs and false prophets performing great miracles, but we have not seen that yet.

What then did Jesus mean in Matthew 24:5?

Understand carefully: Jesus said, "For many shall come in my name, saying, I am Christ; and shall deceive many." Jesus said many would come in his name. They would speak in his name. Jesus said many would say Jesus is the Christ, but they would use it to deceive. Don't all Christians say that Jesus is the Christ? Yes! But do they all speak the truth? Some people have even said, "You can believe anything and be a Christian." Is that true? Jesus said there would be religious deception in his name, by many who would say that Jesus is the Christ. Every Christian group accepts that Jesus is the Christ, but do they all speak the truth? Let Jesus answer that question: "For many shall come in my name, saying, I am Christ; and shall deceive many." Jesus warned his disciples about religious deception, and he gave that warning when they had asked him about his return. In the parallel account in the book of Luke, we read:

> **Luke 21:8** And he said, Take heed that ye be not deceived: for many shall come in my name, saying, I am *Christ*; and the time draweth near: go ye not therefore after them.

Please read that again. How amazing. Jesus said if some say that the time draws near, "go ye not therefore after them." How many preachers have told us that the end-time is near? Jesus said we must not follow them. Can we believe that? Jesus said if they tell us that the time is near, we should not follow them. Yet, preachers have been telling people that for many years. They tell us Jesus will come soon. And Jesus said, that when they say that, do not follow them.

Sometimes, I just have to stop and marvel at the words of Jesus. Here was one who walked the earth two thousand years ago; a carpenter from Nazareth who said many would use his name. What were the chances of that happening? What were the chances of millions of people around the world using his name? And what were the chances of many using his name to deceive? Yet that is what Jesus predicted would happen. Jesus said they would come in his name, they would say Jesus is the Christ, and they would tell you the time of Jesus' return is near. Jesus said: Go not after them!

Jesus continued, in Matthew's account:

> **Matthew 24:6–8** And ye shall hear of wars and rumours of wars: see that ye be not troubled: for all *these things* must come to pass, but the end is not yet. For nation shall rise against nation, and kingdom against kingdom: and there shall be famines, and pestilences, and earthquakes, in divers places. All these *are* the beginning of sorrows.

"Ye shall hear of wars and rumours of wars: see that ye be not troubled" (Matthew 24:6). Is that what preachers have told us? No. To the contrary, they have said, "There are wars and threats of war. We are in trouble. This is the time of the end!" Did Jesus say that wars, famines, and earthquakes were signs of his coming? No. He said that when his disciples saw these things, the disciples need not be troubled, "all these things must come to pass, but the end is not yet"—and the end would still be some time in the future. Jesus said these were only the "beginning of sorrows," or "beginning of birth pains" (NIV). When a pregnant woman starts having contractions, does it mean the baby will arrive immediately? Women might wish that were true. Instead, the baby may not arrive for many long painful hours. Wars, famines, and earthquakes would not be a sign of Jesus' coming. They would only be the beginning of "birth pains."

Let's read the parallel account in the Gospel of Luke:

> **Luke 21:9** But when ye shall hear of wars and commotions,

be not terrified: for these things must first come to pass; but the end *is* not by and by.

Jesus told his disciples not to be terrified when they heard of wars and commotions. Is this what you have been told? No, chances are you have been told, as I have been, and as I continue to hear preachers say, "You'd better be terrified. There are wars, there are pestilences, and now there is AIDS. Jesus may come tonight!" That is not true, for Jesus said: "but the end is not by and by."

Are wars, commotions, famines, and earthquakes signs of the end? No! Anyone who has said that has been mistaken. Think about this: how many wars have occurred since Jesus said those words? In AD 70, the Roman armies under Titus besieged Jerusalem. There was famine and pestilence. The city and the temple were destroyed and many Jews killed. The rest were taken into slavery, but it was not the "time of the end." Wars have continued through the ages, so have famines. There have been many earthquakes. We still have wars and famines and earthquakes. Jesus did not say that wars, famines, and earthquakes were signs of his coming.

During 1914 to 1918 was the "war to end all wars"—World War I. It was the most horrific war humans had ever seen. It was followed by the 1918 flu epidemic that swept around the world and killed millions. It was a time of war and pestilence, but it was not the "time of the end", even though many at the time thought it was.

Since then, we have had World War II, the Korean and Vietnam wars, and many more. We still face war. Millions face famine and starvation and disease epidemics. But are these the signs of the return of Jesus? No, not if we believe the words of Jesus!

Imagine you lived in Europe at the end of World War I. Around you would have been incredible devastation. The war was followed by the flu epidemic. Imagine if a preacher came to you at that time and said, "This is the time of the end. We have war and pestilence," yet on your lap you had a Bible open to the words of Jesus: "But when ye shall hear of wars and commotions, be not terrified: for these things must first come to pass; but the end is not by and by." Whom would you have believed: the preacher or the words of Jesus?

Imagine it was 1945, Germany was now defeated, and you were an Allied soldier who had just arrived at the gates of one of Hitler's concentration camps. You would have seen the horror of half-starved Jews, Poles, and many others, their ribs showing, and their eyes deep in their sockets. You would have seen a pile of bodies destined for the ovens where thousands had already been cremated. The smell of burned flesh would have permeated everything. If, at that time, someone had said to you, "This is the time of the end, nothing could be worse than this," you may have agreed. But the words of Jesus would have said, "But when ye shall hear of wars and commotions, be not terrified: for these things must first come to pass; but the end is not by and by."

Those words of Jesus are still true today. There still are wars and threats of war. There are, and will be, famines, disease, and earthquakes. Are these signs of the end? No. "These things must first come to pass; but the end is not by and by," said Jesus to his disciples on the Mount of Olives.

The Signs of the Times

WE KNOW that Jesus told the disciples, "And ye shall hear of wars and rumours of wars: see that ye be not troubled: for all *these things* must come to pass, but the end is not yet. For nation shall rise against nation, and kingdom against kingdom: and there shall be famines, and pestilences, and earthquakes, in divers places. All these are the beginning of sorrows" (Matthew 24:6–8)

Yes, the world has faced, and will face, terrible things. Man's inventiveness has made wars far worse. Droughts and famines have become worse. The potential for pestilence is worse. Enormous cities are now built on earthquake fault lines. The specter of enormous disaster looms, but we can read the words of Jesus as recorded by Luke: "But when ye shall hear of wars and commotions, be not terrified: for these things must first come to pass; but the end is not by and by" (Luke 21:9).

Will things get worse? The sad answer is, yes. Conditions in this world of ours are still going to get a lot worse. We continue reading in Luke:

> **Luke 21:10–11** Then said he unto them, Nation shall rise against nation, and kingdom against kingdom: And great earthquakes shall be in divers places, and famines, and pestilences; and fearful sights and great signs shall there be from heaven.

Yes, fearful events lie ahead of us, but the end is not yet.

But, some may say, Jesus told us to watch for "the signs of the times!" Yes, Jesus did use that term, but when he used those words, he was *not* talking about his Second Coming! Let me repeat that: when Jesus used the words, "the signs of the times", he was *not* talking about his Second Coming. Let's read it:

> **Matthew 16:1–4** The Pharisees also with the Sadducees came, and tempting desired him that he would shew them a sign from heaven. He answered and said unto them, When it is evening, ye say, *It will be* fair weather: for the sky is red. And in the morning, *It will be* foul weather to day: for the sky is red and lowring. O *ye* hypocrites, ye can discern the face of the sky; but can ye not *discern* the signs of the times? A wicked and adulterous generation seeketh after a sign; and there shall no sign be given unto it, but the sign of the prophet Jonas. And he left them, and departed.

Jesus *did* use the phrase, "the signs of the times," but he was not talking about his return. Jesus was talking to some of the religious leaders of his day. They wanted Jesus to show them some sign from heaven that he was the Christ, the Messiah. Jesus said no sign would be given them but the sign of Jonah. What was the sign of Jonah? Jesus had mentioned this sign in a previous chapter:

> **Matthew 12:38–40** Then certain of the scribes and of the Pharisees answered, saying, Master, we would see a sign from thee. But he answered and said unto them, An evil and adulterous generation seeketh after a sign; and there shall no sign

be given to it, but the sign of the prophet Jonas: For as Jonas was three days and three nights in the whale's belly; so shall the Son of man be three days and three nights in the heart of the earth.

Jesus said the only sign he would give them was the sign of Jonah. Amazingly, they could know that Jesus was the Christ, the Messiah, after his death and resurrection, because Jesus would be in the grave for three days and three nights, just as Jonah had been in the belly of the huge fish: "Now the LORD had prepared a great fish to swallow up Jonah. And Jonah was in the belly of the fish three days and three nights" (Jonah 1:17).

In 1973, I was talking to a Muslim man. He said to me, "Jesus was not the Messiah."

"Why do you say that?" I asked him.

"Jesus was crucified on Good Friday and rose on Sunday morning. Jesus was not in the grave for three days and three nights as he said he would be, so he could not have been the Messiah," he replied.

I explained to him, "You are confusing two different things: what Jesus said and Christian tradition. There is a difference. In Matthew 12:40, Jesus said, 'For as Jonas was three days and three nights in the whale's [fish's] belly; so shall the Son of man be three days and three nights in the heart of the earth.' In Jonah 1:17, we read, 'And Jonah was in the belly of the fish three days and three nights.' These two expressions, one in the New Testament Greek and one in the Old Testament Hebrew, can only mean three days and three nights. When you really understand the events of the New Testament, you will know that what Jesus said was exactly true. He was in the grave for three days and three nights, despite the so-called Christian tradition of a Good Friday crucifixion and an Easter Sunday resurrection."

Then, I learned that the man, who could read the original Hebrew, and had looked up the Greek text, knew very well what I was talking about and had just tried to trip me up, like he had tripped up many other Christians. Unfortunately, far too many Christians have accepted tradition blindly instead of reading and accepting what Jesus said.

Jesus did use the phrase "the signs of the times," but when he used those words, he was talking to the religious leaders of his day who were asking for a sign from heaven. Let's read Matthew 16:1–4 again: "The Pharisees also with the Sadducees came, and tempting desired him that he would shew them a sign from heaven. He answered and said unto them, When it is evening, ye say, *It will be* fair weather: for the sky is red. And in the morning, *It will be* foul weather to day: for the sky is red and lowring. O *ye* hypocrites, ye can discern the face of the sky; but can ye not *discern* the signs of the times? A wicked and adulterous generation seeketh after a sign; and there shall no sign be given unto it, but the sign of the prophet Jonas. And he left them, and departed."

Jesus said to the Jewish leaders of his day that they should have been able to interpret the signs of the times. The signs of that time should have shown them that Jesus was the Messiah, but Jesus was talking about his first coming. Yes, when Jesus used that phrase, he was referring to his first coming, not his return, the Second Coming. We should not confuse what Jesus said to the religious leaders of his day with what he referred to in the Olivet Prophecy in Matthew 24, Mark 13, and Luke 21.

We need to always read the words of Jesus in context. Who was Jesus talking to? What was he talking about, and what did he really say? Now let us continue with Jesus' Olivet Prophecy.

Religious Persecution

WARS, FAMINES, pestilence, and earthquakes have continued from the time of Jesus to our day. They were *not* signs of the end, even though many have mistakenly taken them to be. All we need to do is read and believe what Jesus said.

What about religious persecution? Would religious persecution be a sign of the end? Let's continue reading the words of Jesus in his Olivet Prophecy:

> **Matthew 24:9** Then shall they deliver you up to be afflicted, and shall kill you: and ye shall be hated of all nations for my name's sake.

Persecution of the disciples of Jesus began *then*, very soon after the death and resurrection of Jesus:

> **Acts 7:59–8:3** And they stoned Stephen, calling upon *God*, and saying, Lord Jesus, receive my spirit. And he kneeled down, and cried with a loud voice, Lord, lay not this sin to their charge. And when he had said this, he fell asleep. And Saul was consenting unto his death. And at that time there was a great persecution against the church which was at Jerusalem; and they were all scattered abroad throughout

the regions of Judaea and Samaria, except the apostles. And devout men carried Stephen *to his burial*, and made great lamentation over him. As for Saul, he made havock of the church, entering into every house, and haling men and women committed *them* to prison.

This was shortly after the beginning of the Christian church. The original persecution came from the Jews. Then King Herod (Herod Agrippa I) joined in on the persecution:

Acts 12:1–4 Now about that time Herod the king stretched forth *his* hands to vex certain of the church. And he killed James the brother of John with the sword. And because he saw it pleased the Jews, he proceeded further to take Peter also. (Then were the days of unleavened bread.) And when he had apprehended him, he put *him* in prison, and delivered *him* to four quaternions of soldiers to keep him; intending after [Passover] to bring him forth to the people.

James, one of the original twelve disciples, was killed. Peter was put in prison, from where an angel had to rescue him (Acts 12:5–10). Death and persecution had come on the disciples of Jesus. Was that a sign of the end? Of course not!

The persecution, started by the Jews, was later taken over by the Romans; then greatly intensified when Christians started killing other Christians. We have two thousand years of history, in all its gruesome, gory detail, telling us what happened. Was religious persecution a sign of the end? No! Jesus said persecution would come. The disciples of Jesus would be persecuted and put to death. For almost two thousand years, the disciples of Jesus faced persecution and death, much of it from other "Christians."

Today, some disciples of Jesus still face persecution and death. Is this a sign of the end? No! And the persecution of Jesus' followers by those who think they are doing a service to God will increase before it is all over. Jesus told his disciples, "They shall put you out of the synagogues: yea, the time cometh, that whosoever killeth you will think that he doeth God service" (John 16:2). Persecution against the followers of Jesus did not always come from "pagans." It also came from those who said they worshipped God.

But what about the "great falling away" some have talked about as a sign of the imminent return of Jesus? Surely, some have said, that is a sign of the end. What is the "great falling away"? That is what we need to examine next.

The Great Falling Away

SOME HAVE said that there has to come a great falling away before Jesus will return. They have said that because of what the apostle Paul wrote to the Thessalonians:

2 Thessalonians 2:3 Let no man deceive you by any means: for that day shall not come, except there come a falling away first . . .

Paul was writing about the "day of Christ" (2 Thessalonians. 2:2). He said it would not come until, "there come a falling away first." Paul wrote there would be a falling away—Greek: *apostasia*, an apostasy, from *apo*—away, and *stasis*—a standing: an abandoning of what one has believed in. Christians would leave the faith. We will return to this writing of Paul again later.

What did Jesus say?

Matthew 24:10–13 And then shall many be offended, and shall betray one another, and shall hate one another. And many false prophets shall rise, and shall deceive many. And because iniquity shall abound, the love of many shall wax cold. But he that shall endure unto the end, the same shall be saved.

Would a turning away from the faith be a sign of the end? Did some turn away from the faith in Jesus' day? Yes. We read, "From that *time* many of his disciples went back, and walked no more with him" (John 6:66).

Even before the death of Jesus, some disciples turned back and no longer followed him. Some think there were only the twelve disciples. A disciple is a follower of a teacher, one who is taught by that teacher. Jesus had far more than just the twelve disciples. In Luke 10:1, we read, "After these things the Lord appointed other seventy also, and sent them two and two before his face into every city and place, whither he himself would come." At that time, Jesus sent out seventy disciples. Later, Jesus had many more, but not all of them continued to follow him. Many of them turned back and no longer followed him.

Did people in Paul's day turn away from the faith? Paul wrote, "Holding faith, and a good conscience; which some having put away concerning faith have made shipwreck: Of whom is Hymenaeus and Alexander; whom I have delivered unto Satan, that they may learn not to blaspheme" (1 Timothy 1:19–20).

Some of those who turned away from the faith are mentioned by name. In Colossians 4:14, Paul wrote, "Luke, the beloved physician, and Demas, greet you." Yet in 2 Timothy 4:10, he had to write, "For Demas hath forsaken me, having loved this present world, and is departed unto Thessalonica." He added, "Only Luke is with me." Luke remained faithful, while Demas did not.

In the book of Revelation, there is a letter to the church at Ephesus, one of the churches Paul started. It says, "Nevertheless I have somewhat against thee, because thou hast left thy first love. Remember therefore from whence thou art fallen, and repent, and do the first works; or else I will come unto thee quickly, and will remove thy candlestick out of his place, except thou repent" (Revelation 2:4–5). The wonderful church at Ephesus, the church to whom Paul wrote the book of Ephesians, ceased to exist; it died like so many churches die today. Was this turning away from the faith by so many a sign of Jesus' return? No, it has always happened and is still happening.

Is there going to be a great falling away at the end-time? Yes, that is what Paul wrote to the Thessalonians. Let us read the whole passage:

> **2 Thessalonians 2:1–4** Now we beseech you, brethren, by the coming of our Lord Jesus Christ, and *by* our gathering together unto him, That ye be not soon shaken in mind, or be troubled, neither by spirit, nor by word, nor by letter as from us, as that the day of Christ is at hand. Let no man deceive you by any means: for *that day shall not come*, except there come a falling away first, and that man of sin be revealed, the son of perdition; who opposeth and exalteth himself above all that is called God, or that is worshipped; so that he as God sitteth in the temple of God, shewing himself that he is God.

Has this occurred? Has someone sat in the temple of God saying he is God? Not at all! Today, there is no temple in Jerusalem. Some have speculated that the Jews will rebuild the temple on Mount Moriah next to the Muslim Dome of the Rock. Others have said this man of sin will stand in the church. If so, which church? One thing is clear. Jesus said, "Take heed that no man deceive you" (Matthew 24:4), and Paul wrote, "Let no man deceive you by any means" (2 Thessalonians 2:3). We have to take heed; we have to be careful that no one deceives us. Many things still have to happen before Jesus will return.

Some have said that they have seen a falling away. They see people leaving Christianity or leaving their church. Is that really a sign of the end? No! Paul wrote that a falling away is going to come and a "man of sin" is going to be revealed, one who will stand in God's temple and proclaim himself to be worshipped. Has that happened? No! When it happens, it will be very clear. Paul also wrote:

> **2 Thessalonians 2:8–9** And then shall that Wicked be revealed, whom the Lord shall consume with the spirit of his mouth, and shall destroy with the brightness of his coming: *Even him*, whose coming is after the working of Satan with all power and signs and lying wonders.

This man of sin, who will be revealed, will come, "with all power and signs and lying wonders," and the Lord is going to consume him. That shows it is a future event, a dramatic event that will take place just before the Lord's return.

But, we may say, we can't be deceived we are Christians. Really? This false prophet will come with "all power and signs and lying wonders." Paul continued:

> **2 Thessalonians 2:10** And with all deceivableness of unrighteousness in them that perish; because they received not the love of the truth, that they might be saved.

"They received not the love of the truth," wrote Paul. Don't we all love the truth? Don't we all love the truth of the Bible? What if you find something in the Bible that contradicts what you have always believed? Will you accept it?

Paul continued:

> **2 Thessalonians 2:11–12** And for this cause God shall send them strong delusion, that they should believe a lie: That they all might be damned who believed not the truth, but had pleasure in unrighteousness.

Because they had pleasure in unrighteousness and believed not the truth, God would send them a strong delusion, that they should believe a lie. Could that happen to us? Could we really end up believing a lie? Let's read the words of Jesus again:

> **Matthew 24:10–13** And then shall many be offended, and shall betray one another, and shall hate one another. And many false prophets shall rise, and shall deceive many. And because iniquity shall abound, the love of many shall wax cold. But he that shall endure unto the end, the same shall be saved.

Have people turned away from the faith? Yes. It happened in the past. It is still happening, and it will continue to happen. Have some who were disciples of Jesus betrayed each other and hated each other? Unfortunately, yes! Far too often, so much so that we should ask who were—and are—the true disciples of Jesus.

Have there been false prophets? Yes, there have been, and there will be many more. Has wickedness increased? Yes. Has the love of many grown cold? Yes. Even your love for God and his Word may have grown cold. Do we need to endure unto the end? Yes. Most

Christians have had to endure until they died or were killed. We have to endure even if Jesus does not arrive during our lifetimes.

But is Christians leaving the faith, or their churches, or your church, a sign of the imminent return of Jesus? The simple answer is, no! The question really is whether *we* will remain faithful. Will *our* names one day be recorded as those who remained faithful to the end, or will our names, like those of Hymenaeus, Alexander, and Demas, be written down as those who forsook the faith and did not remain faithful?

When the apostle Paul wrote, "For that day shall not come, except there come a falling away first, and that man of sin be revealed, the son of perdition; who opposeth and exalteth himself above all that is called God, or that is worshipped; so that he as God sitteth in the temple of God, shewing himself that he is God" (2 Thessalonians 2:3–4), he was talking about a far greater event than people leaving their church!

The Sign of the End

SO FAR, we have read the first thirteen verses of Matthew 24. We have seen that religious deception was not a sign of the end. Neither were wars, famines, and earthquakes. Religious persecution was not a sign of the end, nor were people leaving the Christian church. Will there come a falling away, however that may happen, and "a man of sin" be revealed (2 Thessalonians 2:3)? Yes, but it has not happened yet.

Did Jesus say that something would happen, and *then* the end would come? Yes, we must read it, and you may find it quite surprising:

> **Matthew 24:14** And this gospel of the kingdom shall be preached in all the world for a witness unto all nations; and then shall the end come.

What an amazing statement by Jesus. It ends with, "and then shall the end come." This is the first time Jesus said this. These words are definite. Preachers have told us we need to look at wars, famines, pestilence, and earthquakes. These, they have said, are the signs of the end. Jesus said they were not. But how many preachers have told us that what has to happen before Jesus returns is that the gospel of the Kingdom has to be preached to all nations? Not many.

But what is this "gospel of the kingdom"? Think about this: is there a nation on Earth where the name of Jesus has not been preached?

How well I remember a trip I took, in 1964, behind the Iron Curtain. I had traveled through the barbed wire fences and machine gun emplacements of the border between Austria and Hungary. I then traveled through Hungary into Romania. These were Communist countries. How amazed I was to find Christian churches in almost every village in Romania. Every Sunday, scores of people walked to church, Bibles in hand. They knew about Jesus. One Romanian man said he wanted to sing me a song in English. He sang, "Jesus loves me, this I know, for the Bible tells me so." That was the only English he knew. Even way behind the Iron Curtain, people knew about Jesus.

After the Berlin Wall came down and the Iron Curtain was removed, many, in the west, were surprised to find that Christian churches had survived in Communist countries for all those years. Later, when the Bamboo Curtain was lifted, to allow free entry into China, many Christians were found there. For years, they had practiced their religion in secret. Yes, Jesus had been preached in China. Is there a country on Earth where Jesus has not been preached? Hardly!

But notice that Jesus did not say, "When *Jesus* is preached to all nations, then the end will come." Jesus has been preached in all nations. There is hardly a nation on Earth where the name of Jesus is not known. People may not like it. In fact, they may reject it, but the name of Jesus has been heard everywhere. In fact, it is known in far too many places where it is used profanely.

What did Jesus say? He said, "And this gospel of the kingdom shall be preached in all the world for a witness unto all nations; and then shall the end come" (Matthew 24:14). Has the gospel of the Kingdom been preached as a testimony to all nations? What *is* the gospel of the Kingdom?

Let us read about when Jesus started his ministry:

> **Mark 1:14–15** Now after that John was put in prison, Jesus came into Galilee, preaching the gospel of the kingdom of God, and saying, The time is fulfilled, and the kingdom of God is at hand: repent ye, and believe the gospel.

What then is this gospel of the Kingdom? What was the Kingdom Jesus kept talking about?

Here is a simple question: why does Jesus Christ have two names, Jesus and Christ? Are they names like Bob Jones, Mary Williams, or Themba Moloi, with a first name and last name? How can Christians follow Jesus Christ and not know why he has two names? This is important and has everything to do with the gospel of the Kingdom. Let us answer these very simple questions.

Why was Jesus, called Jesus? The answer is that his parents were told to name him Jesus. Let's read the accounts:

> **Matthew 1:18–21** Now the birth of Jesus Christ was on this wise: When as his mother Mary was espoused to Joseph, before they came together, she was found with child of the Holy Ghost. Then Joseph her husband, being a just *man*, and not willing to make her a publick example, was minded to put her away privily. But while he thought on these things, behold, the angel of the Lord appeared unto him in a dream, saying, Joseph, thou son of David, fear not to take unto thee Mary thy wife: for that which is conceived

in her is of the Holy Ghost. And she shall bring forth a son, and thou shalt call his name JESUS: for he shall save his people from their sins.

Joseph was told in a dream to call the child, Jesus. The New Testament was written in the Greek language. Jesus is the Greek form of the Old Testament Hebrew name Joshua, and it means "Savior" or "the Lord will save."

Why was Jesus, called Jesus? Because the angel of God told Joseph in a dream to "call his name JESUS: for he shall save his people from their sins" (Matthew 1:21). Jesus was called Jesus because Jesus means Savior or the Lord will save.

The same instruction was given to Mary, the mother of Jesus, by the angel Gabriel. Mary's cousin, Elizabeth, was pregnant with the one who became John the Baptist:

> **Luke 1:26–31** And in the sixth month [of Elizabeth's pregnancy] the angel Gabriel was sent from God unto a city of Galilee, named Nazareth, to a virgin espoused to a man whose name was Joseph, of the house of David; and the virgin's name *was* Mary. And the angel came in unto her, and said, Hail, *thou that art* highly favoured, the Lord *is* with thee: blessed *art* thou among women. And when she saw *him*, she was troubled at his saying, and cast in her mind what manner of salutation this should be. And the angel said unto her, Fear not, Mary: for thou hast found favour with God. And, behold, thou shalt conceive in thy womb, and bring forth a son, and shalt call his name JESUS.

So, the reason Jesus was so named was that God commanded it

THE SIGN OF THE END 47

and because Jesus means "Savior" and Jesus would "save his people from their sins."

But, the message from Gabriel to Mary continued:

Luke 1:32–33 He shall be great, and shall be called the Son of the Highest: and the Lord God shall give unto him the throne of his father David: And he shall reign over the house of Jacob for ever; and of his kingdom there shall be no end.

Not only would Jesus be the Savior, but God would also give him a throne, the throne of his father David. Let's understand what that means: David became king of Israel about 940 BC. Both Joseph and Mary were descendants of David, so Jesus was born of the royal family of the Jews. However, the last king of the line of David to rule was King Zedekiah of Judah. Zedekiah died in Babylon with no offspring, about six hundred years before the time of Jesus: "And the king of Babylon slew the sons of Zedekiah before his eyes: he slew also all the princes of Judah in Riblah. Then he put out the eyes of Zedekiah; and the king of Babylon bound him in chains, and carried him to Babylon, and put him in prison till the day of his death" (Jeremiah 52:10–11).

Zedekiah's brother, Jechonias (Matthew 1:11), also called Jehoiachin (2 Kings 24:15), was also taken to Babylon: "And it came to pass in the seven and thirtieth year of the captivity of Jehoiachin king of Judah, in the twelfth month, in the five and twentieth *day* of the month, *that* Evil-merodach king of Babylon in the *first* year of his reign lifted up the head of Jehoiachin king of Judah, and brought him forth out of prison, And spake kindly unto him, and set his throne above the throne of the kings that *were* with him in

Babylon, and changed his prison garments: and he did continually eat bread before him all the days of his life" (Jeremiah 52:31–33). That royal family of the Jews continued in Babylon. A grandson of Jechonias, Zerubbabel, returned to Jerusalem with the exiled Jews to rebuild the temple (Ezra 2:1–2).

Mary, the mother of Jesus, was a descendant of Jechonias and Zerubbabel (Matthew 1:12), and therefore a descendant of King David of Israel. Most people do not think about the fact that Jesus was born of the royal family of the Jews, yet, at Christmastime, they may sing, "Once in royal David's city." Bethlehem was the city of David, and Jesus was born there as a descendant of David. Notice again what Gabriel told Mary:

> **Luke 1:32–33** He shall be great, and shall be called the Son of the Highest: and the Lord God shall give unto him the throne of his father David: And he shall reign over the house of Jacob for ever; and of his kingdom there shall be no end.

Not only was Jesus born as the Savior, he was born to be king. The Lord God said that Jesus would reign over the house of Jacob forever. He would be a king forever, and he would have a kingdom that would never end!

Think about it. Because of the decree of Caesar Augustus—the emperor of the Roman Empire, the most powerful ruler in the world at that time—a Jew of Nazareth, Joseph, took his pregnant wife, Mary, to Bethlehem for the taxing. Why? Bethlehem was the city of David, and Mary and Joseph, descendants of David, had to go there. This taxing required all to return to their hometowns. That is how the prophecy was fulfilled that Jesus was to be born in

Bethlehem, "But thou, Beth-lehem Ephratah, *though* thou be little among the thousands of Judah, *yet* out of thee shall he come forth unto me *that is* to be ruler in Israel; whose goings forth *have been* from of old, from everlasting" (Micah 5:2). Bethlehem was the city of David. Both Joseph and Mary were descendants of David. David was king of Israel, which means that Jesus was born of a royal family. Someone born of a royal family could be king!

Remember what the wise men said when they came looking for Jesus, "Where is he that is born King of the Jews?" (Matthew 2:2). Herod, a king who was not of the line of David, a foreigner who had been placed in position by the Romans, did not know the prophecies: "When Herod the king had heard *these things*, he was troubled, and all Jerusalem with him. And when he had gathered all the chief priests and scribes of the people together, he demanded of them where Christ should be born. And they said unto him, In Bethlehem of Judaea: for thus it is written by the prophet" (Matthew 2:3–5).

The wise men were looking for a king. Did you notice what Herod asked? He asked the chief priest and the scribes of the Jews where the "Christ" was to be born! What does "Christ" mean? It means "the Anointed One." Notice what the followers of Jesus said in Acts 4:26: "The kings of the earth stood up, and the rulers were gathered together against the Lord, and against his Christ." They were quoting from Psalm 2:2: "The kings of the earth set themselves, and the rulers take counsel together, against the LORD, and against his anointed." This is a simple way to prove, from the Bible, that Christ means Anointed.

We also read in John 1:41, "He [Andrew] first findeth his own brother Simon, and saith unto him, We have found the Messias [Greek form of *Messiah*], which is, being interpreted, the Christ."

The Greek word *Christ* has the same meaning as the Hebrew word *Messiah*—"the Anointed One." But what does all of this have to do with the gospel of the Kingdom? Please keep reading.

Jesus was called "Christ" from birth:

Luke 2:8–11 And there were in the same country shepherds abiding in the field, keeping watch over their flock by night. And, lo, the angel of the Lord came upon them, and the glory of the Lord shone round about them: and they were sore afraid. And the angel said unto them, Fear not: for, behold, I bring you good tidings of great joy, which shall be to all people. For unto you is born this day in the city of David a Saviour, which is Christ the Lord.

So, from birth Jesus was the Christ. But why was Jesus called Christ, the Anointed One? In the Old Testament, the high priest was anointed into office:

Leviticus 8:12 [Moses] poured of the anointing oil upon Aaron's head, and anointed him, to sanctify him.

What does that have to do with Jesus? Aaron, the high priest, was the one who went to God on behalf of the people of Israel. In the New Testament, we are told, "Wherefore, holy brethren, partakers of the heavenly calling, consider the Apostle and High Priest of our profession, Christ Jesus" (Hebrews 3:1). An apostle is one who is sent. Jesus was sent to Earth to preach the gospel and to die. That is why he is our Apostle. But, Jesus is also our High Priest. In the Old Testament, the high priest went to God on behalf of the people. In the New Testament, we are told to pray "in Jesus' name."

Jesus said, "And whatsoever ye shall ask in my name, that will I do, that the Father may be glorified in the Son. If ye shall ask any thing in my name, I will do *it*" (John 14:13–14). Why do we pray in Jesus' name? Because Jesus is at the right hand of God the Father, interceding for us. Jesus is our great High Priest in heaven. Notice one very encouraging scripture:

> **Hebrews 4:14–16** Seeing then that we have a great high priest, that is passed into the heavens, Jesus the Son of God, let us hold fast *our* profession. For we have not an high priest which cannot be touched with the feeling of our infirmities; but was in all points tempted like as *we are, yet* without sin. Let us therefore come boldly unto the throne of grace, that we may obtain mercy, and find grace to help in time of need.

Jesus is the Anointed One, the Christ, because he is our anointed High Priest in heaven. How wonderful!

But, who else in the Old Testament was anointed into office? Answer: the kings of Israel!

> **1 Samuel 16:13** Then Samuel took the horn of oil, and anointed him in the midst of his brethren: and the spirit of the LORD came upon David from that day forward.

The kings of Israel were anointed into office. Why is that important? Because Jesus came not only to be our Savior and our High Priest, but also to be King! That is why he came from the kingly line of David. Let us repeat what the angel, Gabriel, said to Mary: "And, behold, thou shalt conceive in thy womb, and bring forth a son, and shalt call his name Jesus. He shall be great, and shall be called the Son of the Highest: and the Lord God shall give unto him the throne of his father David: And he shall reign over the house of Jacob for ever; and of his kingdom there shall be no end" (Luke 1:31–33).

When Jesus stood before Pontius Pilate: "Pilate therefore said unto him, Art thou a king then? Jesus answered, Thou sayest that I am a king. To this end was I born, and for this cause came I into the world, that I should bear witness unto the truth. Every one that is of the truth heareth my voice" (John 18:37). Jesus was born to be King!

Jesus was called Christ, the Anointed One, the Messiah, because he was born to be King, and he is going to be KING OF KINGS (Revelation 19:16), and he is coming to rule on this earth!

Notice more verses in the book of Hebrews:

Hebrew 1:8–9 But unto the Son he saith, Thy throne, O God, is for ever and ever: a sceptre of righteousness is the sceptre of thy kingdom. Thou hast loved righteousness, and hated iniquity; therefore God, even thy God, hath anointed thee with the oil of gladness above thy fellows.

Jesus Christ has two names. Why? Because he is the Savior, *Jesus*, and he is the *Christ*, the Anointed One, the Messiah, our High Priest and the coming King of kings! And Jesus said, "And this gospel of the kingdom shall be preached in all the world for a witness unto all nations; and then shall the end come" (Matthew 24:14).

What is the gospel of the Kingdom? The word "gospel", which you can check in any Bible dictionary or study Bible, comes from an Old English word, *godspel*, which means "good news." The Greek word is *euangelium,* from which we get the word *evangelist*—one who brings good news.

Jesus Christ has two names. He is called, Jesus Christ, or Christ Jesus, or Jesus the Christ. Why? Because he is both Savior—*Jesus,* and Messiah—*Christ.*

What is the gospel of the Kingdom? It is the good news that Jesus, the Christ, who died for us as our Savior, is now in heaven as our High Priest, and is coming back to rule this world as King of kings, and, as Gabriel told Mary, "of his kingdom there shall be no end." It is the same good news that was predicted by all the Old Testament prophets and described so vividly by the prophet Isaiah:

> **Isaiah 2:1–4** The word that Isaiah the son of Amoz saw concerning Judah and Jerusalem. And it shall come to pass in the last days, *that* the mountain of the Lord's house shall be established in the top of the mountains, and shall be exalted above the hills; and all nations shall flow unto it. And many people shall go and say, Come ye, and let us go up to the mountain of the Lord to the house of the God of Jacob; and he will teach us of his ways, and we will walk in his paths: for out of Zion shall go forth the law, and the word of the Lord from Jerusalem. And he shall judge among the nations, and shall rebuke many people: and they shall beat their swords into plowshares, and their spears into pruninghooks: nation shall not lift up sword against nation, neither shall they learn war any more.

> **Isaiah 11:1–9** And there shall come forth a rod out of the stem of Jesse [the father of David]; and a Branch shall grow

out of his roots: And the spirit of the Lord shall rest upon him, the spirit of wisdom and understanding, the spirit of counsel and might, the spirit of knowledge and of the fear of the Lord; And shall make him of quick understanding in the fear of the Lord: and he shall not judge after the sight of his eyes, neither reprove after the hearing of his ears: But with righteousness shall he judge the poor, and reprove with equity for the meek of the earth: and he shall smite the earth with the rod of his mouth, and with the breath of his lips shall he slay the wicked. And righteousness shall be the girdle of his loins, and faithfulness the girdle of his reins. The wolf also shall dwell with the lamb, and the leopard shall lie down with the kid; and the calf and the young lion and the fatling together; and a little child shall lead them. And the cow and the bear shall feed; their young ones shall lie down together: and the lion shall eat straw like the ox. And the sucking child shall play on the hole of the asp, and the weaned child shall put his hand on the cockatrice' den. They shall not hurt nor destroy in all my holy mountain: for the earth shall be full of the knowledge of the Lord, as the waters cover the sea.

As we have seen before, the book of Revelation pictures a future time when the saints "lived and reigned with Christ a thousand years" (Revelation 20:4). To Thyatira, one of the seven churches of Revelation, Jesus said, "And he that overcometh, and keepeth my works unto the end, to him will I give power over the nations" (Revelation 2:26).

In Revelation 5:10, we read, "And hast made us unto our God kings and priests: and we shall reign on the earth."

To his disciples Jesus said, "Verily I say unto you, That ye which have followed me, in the regeneration when the Son of man shall sit in the throne of his glory, ye also shall sit upon twelve thrones, judging the twelve tribes of Israel" (Matthew 19:28).

And in the Olivet Prophecy Jesus said, "And this gospel of the kingdom shall be preached in all the world for a witness unto all nations; and then shall the end come" (Matthew 24:14).

What is the gospel of the Kingdom? It is the good news that Jesus, who died for us as the Savior of mankind, is going to return to this earth to rule the earth with his saints and bring peace to the nations. It is a glorious message, a message of hope to all mankind.

Is the gospel of the Kingdom being preached in the whole world as a testimony to all nations? Not at all! Some of you have never understood why Jesus has two names or why he was born to be King. What about the rest of the world? Yes, many have preached Jesus. They have talked about Jesus as our Savior, but what about the gospel, the good news, of the Kingdom? The Kingdom is mentioned more than a hundred times in the New Testament. Matthew generally calls it the "kingdom of heaven," because it will come from heaven, except in Matthew 6:33, 12:28 19:24, 21:31, and 21:43, where he uses "kingdom of God." Mark, Luke, and John call it the Kingdom of God. It is the same thing. It will come from heaven when Jesus returns. Jesus will be King of kings (Revelation 19:16). It is the time when "the kingdoms of this world are become *the kingdoms* of our Lord, and of his Christ; and he shall reign for ever and ever" (Revelation 11:15). That is the good news of the gospel, and Jesus said that when that gospel, the gospel of the Kingdom, is preached to all nations, the end will come. Has it happened? Many still have no idea what the gospel of the Kingdom of God really means. Some nations have only recently opened their borders to foreign influence, and some nations still outlaw any Christian preaching. Can we really go to every nation on Earth and say, "You heard the gospel of the kingdom preached in your nation as a witness to you, loudly and clearly!"? No!

Many are preaching Jesus as Savior. The name of Jesus is known everywhere. Some have preached, and some continue to preach, the gospel of the Kingdom, but Jesus said, "And this gospel of the kingdom shall be preached in all the world for a witness unto all nations [and notice] and then shall the end come." Surely if the gospel of the Kingdom has been preached to all nations as a witness, the end would have come. Have all nations heard the gospel of the Kingdom? Not yet!

How will the gospel of the Kingdom be preached to the whole world? I do not know. It is not happening today. A few evangelists and churches do preach the gospel of the Kingdom, but certainly not loudly and clearly to all nations. Again, in Revelation 11:15, we read, "The kingdom of the world has become the kingdom of our Lord and of his Christ, and he will reign for ever and ever." In the context of that chapter in Revelation, it is after the time of God's "two witnesses" (Revelation 11:3). Their "testimony" (Revelation 11:7) will last for 1,260 days, after which they will be killed. Will the two witnesses preach the gospel of the Kingdom in the whole world as a testimony to all nations? It seems so. When the two witnesses do their work "they that dwell upon the earth" (Revelation 11:10), will know about it. Then we read, "The kingdom of the world has become the kingdom of our Lord and of his Christ, and he will reign for ever and ever" (Revelation 11:15). How will we know who the two witnesses will be? "And I will give *power* unto my two witnesses, and they shall prophesy a thousand two hundred and threescore days, clothed in sackcloth . . . And if any man will hurt them, fire proceedeth out of their mouth, and devoureth their enemies: and if any man will hurt them, he must in this manner be killed. These have power to shut the heaven, that it rain not in the days of their prophecy: and have power over waters to turn them to blood, and to smite the earth with all plagues, as often as they will" (Revelation 11:3–6). There will be no mistaking these servants of God. Some have claimed that they were the two witnesses, or one of the two witnesses. Their claim was false, as time will tell.

The gospel of the Kingdom has to be preached to all nations; then the end will come. That is what Jesus said. Jesus is going to return as King of kings (Revelation 19:16). Can we imagine the King of kings returning without it being announced to the world in great power and might just before he returns? No, the return of Jesus the Christ will be announced to the world, loudly and clearly, *then* the King of kings will return. As Jesus said in Matthew 24:14, "And this gospel of the kingdom shall be preached in all the world for a witness unto all nations and then shall the end come."

The Abomination of Desolation

JESUS SAID, "And this gospel of the kingdom shall be preached in all the world for a witness unto all nations and then shall the end come" (Matthew 24:14). Let us continue with the words of Jesus in the Olivet Prophecy. We are now reading about the real end-time events:

> **Matthew 24:15** When ye therefore shall see the abomination of desolation, spoken of by Daniel the prophet, stand in the holy place, (whoso readeth, let him understand:)

Jesus said, "Whoso readeth, let him understand." Do you understand exactly what that verse means? I don't! I have read all the prophecies of Daniel about "an abomination that makes desolate" that would come. Let us look at Daniel's prophecies:

> **Daniel 9:26–27** And after threescore and two weeks shall Messiah be cut off, but not for himself: and the people of the prince that shall come shall destroy the city and the sanctuary; and the end thereof *shall be* with a flood, and unto the end of the war desolations are determined. And he shall confirm the covenant with many for one week: and in the midst of the week he shall cause the sacrifice and the

oblation to cease, and for the overspreading of abominations he shall make *it* desolate, even until the consummation, and that determined shall be poured upon the desolate.

Daniel 11:31 And arms shall stand on his part, and they shall pollute the sanctuary of strength, and shall take away the daily *sacrifice*, and they shall place the abomination that maketh desolate.

Daniel 12:11-12 And from the time *that* the daily *sacrifice* shall be taken away, and the abomination that maketh desolate set up, *there shall be* a thousand two hundred and ninety days. Blessed *is* he that waiteth, and cometh to the thousand three hundred and five and thirty days.

Those are the prophecies in the book of Daniel about the abomination of desolation, or the abomination that makes desolate. What does it all mean? Jesus said, "Whoso reads, let him understand." Do you understand? I must admit, I have read many speculations about these prophecies, but I do not understand all that the prophet Daniel wrote.

Without getting into a great technical discussion, let us look at what we can understand:

In 168 BC, Antiochus Epiphanies, a Greek military ruler, came into Jerusalem, killed many Jews, and sacrificed swine's flesh on the altar in the temple and put a pagan idol in the temple. The Jews of Jesus' day knew what Antiochus had done as the "abomination of desolation." This happened before Jesus' time. But Jesus pointed to a future fulfillment of Daniel's prophecy.

We know the Roman general, Titus, destroyed Jerusalem in

AD 70. In the parallel account in Luke, Jesus said, "When you see Jerusalem being surrounded by armies, you will know that its desolation is near" (Luke 21:20). That was certainly true in AD 70, but there is no historical account of "an abomination that makes desolate" in AD 70. Will there be a future fulfillment of Daniel's prophecy? Yes, Jesus said so. Is it happening now? No! What we see in Jerusalem and Palestine right now is conflict between Jews and Palestinians, a continual conflict that has gone on since the state of Israel was established in 1948.

Will "Jerusalem being surrounded by armies" be the sign of Jesus' return? Ask yourself, how many times have armies surrounded Jerusalem since Jesus said those words? In AD 70, Titus surrounded Jerusalem with his Roman armies, and then destroyed the city. Jerusalem was destroyed, but it was not the end of the world. The armies of Islam surrounded and took over Jerusalem in about AD 600. In about AD 1000, the Christian crusaders came into Jerusalem, as did General Allenby with the British forces in 1917 during World War I, when Jerusalem was liberated from the Ottoman Empire. All these armies surrounded Jerusalem, but it was not the end of the world.

The modern state of Israel saw wars in 1948, 1956, 1967, and 1973. Were any of these wars the sign of end of the world? No. The modern nation of Israel continues to face war on all fronts.

But Jesus did say, "When ye therefore shall see the abomination of desolation, spoken of by Daniel the prophet, stand in the holy place, (whoso readeth, let him understand:)" (Matthew 24:15). There will be a future fulfillment of Daniel's prophecy when someone stands in Jerusalem and causes the abomination of desolation.

Please note a prophecy we have read before, a prophecy the

apostle Paul wrote to the Thessalonians referring to the time of the return of Jesus:

> **2 Thessalonians 2:1–4** Now we beseech you, brethren, by the coming of our Lord Jesus Christ, and *by* our gathering together unto him, That ye be not soon shaken in mind, or be troubled, neither by spirit, nor by word, nor by letter as from us, as that the day of Christ is at hand. Let no man deceive you by any means: for *that day shall not come*, except there come a falling away first, and that man of sin be revealed, the son of perdition; who opposeth and exalteth himself above all that is called God, or that is worshipped; so that he as God sitteth in the temple of God, shewing himself that he is God.

We have referred to this amazing prophecy before. Paul wrote that the day of Christ will not come until a "man of sin be revealed, the son of perdition; who opposeth and exalteth himself above all that is called God, or that is worshipped; so that he as God sitteth in the temple of God, shewing himself that he is God." If this were not in the Bible, one might think this is science fiction. But it is not. When it happens, there will be no doubt.

In Luke's account, we read:

> **Luke 21:20** And when ye shall see Jerusalem compassed with armies, then know that the desolation thereof is nigh.

As said before, armies have surrounded Jerusalem many times, but it was not the time of the end. Will there be a time when armies will surround Jerusalem and its destruction will again be near? Yes!

There has been so much speculation about Jesus' prophecy of the abomination of desolation. Let us recap what we know for certain:

1. In 168 BC, Antiochus Epiphanies, came into Jerusalem, killed many Jews, and sacrificed swine's flesh on the altar in the temple and put a pagan idol in the temple. The Jews of Jesus' day knew what Antiochus had done as the "abomination of desolation." Jesus spoke of a future fulfillment of the same prophecies in Daniel.

2. Antiochus was a "king of the north" (Daniel 11:29–31); ruling over what was originally part of the Greek Empire of Alexander the Great. The Greek Empire was taken over by the Roman Empire. Titus, who destroyed Jerusalem in AD 70, was a general under the Roman Emperor Vespasian.

3. The Roman Empire, after its collapse in AD 476, was resurrected as the Holy Roman Empire and was ruled over by several successive kings who were crowned by the pope: Justinian, Charlemagne, Otto the Great, Charles the Great, and Napoleon (it is true that Napoleon took the crown from the pope and crowned himself). Then we had Hitler's Third Reich, an attempt to unify Europe by military means.

4. Daniel wrote, "And the king shall do according to his will; and he shall exalt himself, and magnify himself above every god, and shall speak marvellous things against the God of

gods, and shall prosper till the indignation be accomplished: for that that is determined shall be done" (Daniel 11:36). We can compare this to what Paul wrote in 2 Thessalonians 2:3–4: "Let no man deceive you by any means: for *that day shall not come*, except there come a falling away first, and that man of sin be revealed, the son of perdition; who opposeth and exalteth himself above all that is called God, or that is worshipped; so that he as God sitteth in the temple of God, shewing himself that he is God."

With all these points in mind, we need to make sure to heed Paul's warning, "Let no man deceive you by any means" (2 Thessalonians 2:3), and the words of Jesus, "Take heed that no man deceive you" (Matthew 24:4). How can those who are the disciples of Jesus be deceived? By not realizing that not all those who have come "in the name of Jesus" were really speaking *for* Jesus. We have had two thousand years of history since the time of Jesus. Much of that time was filled with persecution and warfare emanating from a Christian Europe. We have had crusades against the infidels, the Muslims, as well as against other Christians. There were times in history when Jews were safer in Arab lands than in Christian countries. Hitler's Third Reich tried to find the "final solution" for the "Jewish problem." It resulted in six million Jews being killed in concentration camps and gas chambers. We do not like to think about it, but six million Jews were put to death in "Christian" Europe.

Who will fulfill the prophecy of Jesus when he said, "When ye therefore shall see the abomination of desolation, spoken of by Daniel the prophet, stand in the holy place, (whoso readeth, let him understand:)" (Matthew 24:15)? We do not know, but we do know where to look. It will not be the Muslims, or the Russians, or the Chinese. The fulfillment of Jesus' prophecy will come from an area most Christian readers of the Bible will least expect. The fulfillment will come from Europe, and it will come from Christian Europe! (Please read my forthcoming book, *Understanding the Book of Revelation*).

Jesus continued, in Matthew's account:

> **Matthew 24:16–20** Then let them which be in Judaea flee into the mountains: Let him which is on the housetop not come down to take any thing out of his house: Neither let him which is in the field return back to take his clothes. And woe unto them that are with child, and to them that give suck in those days! But pray ye that your flight be not in the winter, neither on the sabbath day:

People have had to flee from Judea far too many times, and it will happen again. What Jesus warned is that when this happens, there will not even be enough time for someone in Judea to go into his home to save anything. It will be a dreadful time. Pregnant women and nursing mothers will suffer terribly.

Jesus said they should pray that their flight does not take place on the Sabbath. The original disciples of Jesus observed the Sabbath. Religious Jews in Jerusalem still observe the Sabbath. We read of Jesus, who, "came to Nazareth, where he had been brought up: and, as his custom was, he went into the synagogue on the Sabbath day, and stood up for to read" (Luke 4:16), and of the apostle Paul who, "as his manner was, went in unto them, and three Sabbath days reasoned with them out of the scriptures" (Acts 17:2). It is also still the custom of many Christians today to observe the Saturday Sabbath.

I realize most of Christianity does not observe the seventh-day Sabbath. Most Christian churches have followed the Emperor Constantine's declaration, in AD 321, "Let all judges and townspeople and occupations of all trades rest on the Venerable Day of the Sun [Sunday]" (The Code of Justinian, Book 111, title 12, law 3). Hence most Christians worship on *Sun*day. Does it make a difference? Jesus, when focusing on the end-time events, told his followers to pray that they would not have to flee on the Sabbath.

Has the abomination of desolation been set up in Jerusalem? No! Is there any indication of it being set up soon? I have heard many speculations about these prophecies of Daniel, but I see no sign of them being fulfilled yet. During the first Gulf War, I heard preachers speculate that this heralded the end-time. Now, with the United States and some of its allies embroiled in the second Gulf War, some preachers are proclaiming that this is the event that will lead us to the return of Jesus. Some who used to focus on Saddam Hussein and Iraq are now pointing to Iran. "Iran will join with Russia, and this will lead to the time of the end," a prominent preacher proclaimed recently on television. Jesus said, "Take heed that no man deceive you" (Matthew 24:4). We need to take heed; we must be very careful that no one deceives us.

Since 1917, when General Allenby liberated Jerusalem and Jews started returning to Palestine, some said that was a sign of the end. For almost a hundred years, Jews have been returning to Palestine, but the end has not come. The prophecies these preachers looked at were prophecies of a future exodus at the time of Jesus' return: "Therefore, behold, the days come, saith the LORD, that it shall no more be said, The LORD liveth, that brought up the children of Israel out of the land of Egypt; but, The LORD liveth, that brought up the children of Israel from the land of the north, and from all the lands whither he had driven them: and I will bring them again into their land that I gave unto their fathers" (Jeremiah 16:14. See also Jeremiah 23:8, 31:8, and Isaiah 11:11). This great future exodus will totally dwarf what happened under Moses. Notice when it will happen: "And it shall come to pass in that day, *that* the great trumpet shall be blown, and they shall come which were ready to perish in the land of Assyria, and the outcasts in the land of Egypt, and shall worship the LORD in the holy mount at Jerusalem" (Isaiah 27:13). That future exodus will start *when*, not before, the great trumpet blows that will herald the return of Jesus Christ.

Did Jesus say the return of the Jews to Palestine would be a sign of the end? No! Jesus said that at the end, before his return, Jews would have to flee from Jerusalem and Judea!

The Great Tribulation

I**T SHOULD** already be clear to us that much still has to happen before Jesus will return. That does not mean we can just relax and take it easy. No, we have to be alert and be ready always. History reminds us that things can happen very speedily. In 1933, Hitler came to power as chancellor of Germany. At that time very few saw him as the great enemy. On September 30, 1938, British Prime Minister, Neville Chamberlain, came back from a meeting with Hitler, waved a signed document and proclaimed, "Peace for our time." By 1940, barely two years later, Hitler had conquered most of Europe. Events can change very quickly. The apostle Paul wrote, "But of the times and the seasons, brethren, ye have no need that I write unto you. For yourselves know perfectly that the day of the Lord so cometh as a thief in the night. For when they shall say, Peace and safety; then sudden destruction cometh upon them, as travail upon a woman with child; and they shall not escape. But ye, brethren, are not in darkness, that that day should overtake you as a thief" (1 Thessalonians 5:1–4). We do not have to be in darkness. We can be awake. Paul continued, in verses 5–6, "Ye are all the children of light, and the children of the day: we are not of the night, nor of darkness. Therefore let us not sleep, as do others; but let us watch and be sober."

Now, notice the very important words of Jesus as we continue through the Olivet Prophecy:

Matthew 24:21–22 For then shall be great tribulation, such as was not since the beginning of the world to this time, no, nor ever shall be. And except those days should be shortened, there should no flesh be saved: but for the elect's sake those days shall be shortened.

"For then," said Jesus. When is "then?" When the abomination of desolation of Matthew 24:15 stands in the holy place and people have to flee (Matthew 24:20), there "shall be great tribulation" such as never was, never to be equaled again. Can we believe that?

Look around today. Are things bad? It depends where you are. Maybe they are very bad for you. But, is this the worst time that mankind has ever been through? Never! Of course there are parts of the world that are terrible. There are countries where living conditions are so dreadful most of us are thankful that we do not have to live there. But many countries are doing well. Some nations are enjoying the highest standard of living they have ever known. Do we really see a great tribulation—such as was not since the beginning of the world to this time—according to Jesus' statement? Is that what it is like where you live? I doubt it. It is still going to get far worse before Jesus returns.

No, we are not yet in the great tribulation. That still lies ahead of us, but it will come. These wonderful countries in which we now live are not going to remain this way. Things are going to change for the worse. When we read history, or listen to our elders who might have lived through dreadful times, or watch TV and see what is going on in some of the more desperate countries in the world, it is hard to believe that Jesus said there is going to come "great tribulation, such as was not since the beginning of the world to this time, no, nor ever shall be." It is almost impossible to believe that our countries are going to end up like that. But that is what Jesus said. When that time arrives, we will all know that the great tribulation has come.

"And except those days should be shortened, there should no flesh be saved" (Matthew 24:22). This was Jesus speaking almost two thousand years ago. He predicted a time when, unless God intervenes and cuts the time short, "no flesh [would] be saved." This world is already in survival mode. Can we survive without fossil fuels, the oil and coal that power most of what we do? Can we survive pollution and global warming? Can we survive a nuclear conflagration? No, we can't, unless God intervenes for us!

"But for the elect's sake those days shall be shortened"—that is our only hope, and the good news, the gospel, is that God will send his Son, Jesus Christ, back to this earth as the King of kings and Savior of mankind. The world will be saved, nations will be saved, fauna and flora will be saved, and people will be saved. This is the good news that needs to be preached to the world, and *will* be preached to the world, but as the servants of God proclaim this good news to the world, the servants of Satan the devil, the one "which deceiveth the whole world" (Revelation 12:9), will also be very active. Jesus continued:

> **Matthew 24:23–24** Then [when there will be great tribulation] if any man shall say unto you, Lo, here *is* Christ, or there; believe *it* not. For there shall arise false Christs, and false prophets, and shall shew great signs and wonders; insomuch that, if *it were* possible, they shall deceive the very elect.

If someone came to you, today, and told you that Jesus was

somewhere on the earth, chances are you would shrug it off as a report from some crackpot. But, when things get so desperate on this earth that most people are in utter despair and don't know where to turn, false Christs and false prophets will arise and people will run after them. Jesus said that even the elect, those called out by God himself, would be deceived, if that were possible. Some have said this means it is impossible for the elect to be deceived. I have seen so many people who were Christians for years, who called themselves the elect of God, reject everything they believed, and that was without a great tribulation, or false Christs and false prophets. Don't be so sure that you cannot be deceived.

How can we make sure we are not deceived? By remembering what Jesus said. We don't have to be deceived. Those of us who have been deceived in the past can become undeceived: "Then said Jesus to those Jews which believed on him, If ye continue in my word, *then* are ye my disciples indeed; and ye shall know the truth, and the truth shall make you free" (John 8:32). The words of Jesus are the truth. We can read his words, and we can believe and accept them. We can start living by the words of Jesus. His words are the truth that can make us free.

Jesus warned his disciples, and he warns us, in the next verses:

Matthew 24:25–26 Behold, I have told you before. Wherefore if they shall say unto you, Behold, he is in the desert; go not forth: behold, *he is* in the secret chambers; believe *it* not.

Even when there are some who will perform great miracles, we do not have to be deceived, and we won't be deceived as long as we believe and trust in the plain words that Jesus Christ spoke. But this is much easier said than done.

Take a moment to think about the world in which we live. Most people on Earth are not Christians, and most Christians are nominal Christians—Christians in name only. How many of us are truly committed to living by the teachings of Jesus? Let Jesus answer: "Nevertheless when the Son of man cometh, shall he find faith on the earth?" (Luke 18:8). Did Jesus not know that in the twenty-first century there would be two billion Christians on Earth and thousands of churches? Obviously, Jesus knew something we may not. True faith, according to his words, will be a rarity on Earth when he returns.

Let's read a few more of Jesus' warnings:

> **Matthew 7:13–14** Enter ye in at the strait gate: for wide *is* the gate, and broad *is* the way, that leadeth to destruction, and many there be which go in thereat: Because strait *is* the gate, and narrow *is* the way, which leadeth unto life, and few there be that find it.

Are those words of Jesus really true? Is it really true that only a few find the road that leads to eternal life? He continued:

> **Matthew 7:15–20** Beware of false prophets, which come to you in sheep's clothing, but inwardly they are ravening wolves. Ye shall know them by their fruits. Do men gather grapes of thorns, or figs of thistles? Even so every good tree bringeth forth good fruit; but a corrupt tree bringeth forth evil fruit. A good tree cannot bring forth evil fruit, neither *can* a corrupt tree bring forth good fruit. Every tree

that bringeth not forth good fruit is hewn down, and cast into the fire. Wherefore by their fruits ye shall know them.

How many times does Jesus warn us about false prophets? How will we recognize them? By their fruits, he said. It is so easy for them to use the name of Jesus, but their deeds will turn out not to be the same as the deeds of Jesus, and their words will turn out to be contrary to the words of Jesus. Jesus said:

> **Matthew 7:21–23** Not every one that saith unto me, Lord, Lord, shall enter into the kingdom of heaven; but he that doeth the will of my Father which is in heaven. Many will say to me in that day, Lord, Lord, have we not prophesied in thy name? and in thy name have cast out devils? and in thy name done many wonderful works? And then will I profess unto them, I never knew you: depart from me, ye that work iniquity.

Can some prophesy, drive out demons, even perform miracles in the name of Jesus and still be cast away by Jesus because they are evildoers? It does not seem possible, but Jesus said, "And then will I profess unto them, I never knew you: depart from me, ye that work iniquity." Iniquity means lawlessness. We cannot be a law unto ourselves, deciding for ourselves what we think is right. We should remind ourselves of the words of Jesus: "But if thou wilt enter into life, keep the commandments" (Matthew 19:17).

How then can you know where you stand? How can you be certain of your future? Jesus said:

> **Matthew 7:24–25** Therefore whosoever heareth these

sayings of mine, and doeth them, I will liken him unto a wise man, which built his house upon a rock: and the rain descended, and the floods came, and the winds blew, and beat upon that house; and it fell not: for it was founded upon a rock.

So many times I have asked, what did Jesus say? Why is it important to us? Because, if we hear the words of Jesus and put them into practice, it doesn't matter what happens to us. Our foundation will always be on a rock, and our Rock is Christ (1 Corinthians 10:4).

Jesus continued:

Matthew 7:26–27 And every one that heareth these sayings of mine, and doeth them not, shall be likened unto a foolish man, which built his house upon the sand: And the rain descended, and the floods came, and the winds blew, and beat upon that house; and it fell: and great was the fall of it.

How important are the words of Jesus to you? When last did you open your Bible and read the words of Jesus? To read and heed them is the only hope you have. It is your future!

In 1998, I was challenged to go back and read every word that Jesus spoke. I had a red-letter Bible; a Bible in which every word Jesus spoke is in red letters, a gift to me from one of the congregations I started in South Africa. I went through the Gospels and read every word Jesus spoke. When I finished the Gospels, I went to the book of Revelation, where we also find words Jesus spoke. It was a profound experience. At that time, I had been a Christian for thirty-six years, but the words of Jesus still had an amazing effect on my mind. Those were the same words I first read in 1959, before I truly became a Christian. The words of Jesus had not changed.

When the year 2000 came, I went back to the words of Jesus to answer the question, "Why has Jesus not returned?" This book is a result of that. If you get nothing else out of this book, I trust it will inspire you to go back and read every word Jesus spoke that was recorded for us. Let your life, and your future, be based on the words Jesus spoke! Even when false Christs, and false prophets arise and perform "great signs and wonders" (Matthew 24:24), you wont be deceived. Even when some say, "Behold, he is in the desert," or, "Behold, *he is* in the secret chambers" (Matthew 24:26), you do not have to believe it. And you will not believe a lie, if you make sure that you are always guided by the words of Jesus.

How Will Jesus Return?

WE HAVE read so much about the events that still have to take place before Jesus will return. Now we can find out how Jesus will return.

Let's remind ourselves that we are still reading the words Jesus spoke when he was sitting on the Mount of Olives. That is where the disciples had asked him, "Tell us, when shall these things be? and what shall be the sign of thy coming, and of the end of the world?" (Matthew 24:3). Step by step, Jesus went through all the events his disciples would see through the ages. Then he started talking about his actual return.

> **Matthew 24:27** For as the lightning cometh out of the east, and shineth even unto the west; so shall also the coming of the Son of man be.

What does that mean? There are two explanations that are used. The first is that Jesus was talking about lightning, as in a thunderstorm. The other is that he was talking about the sun lightening the earth, hence the wording, "cometh out of the east, and shineth even unto the west." Jesus' return will not be just a flash in the sky. If you are on earth at that time, you will be able to look up at the sky and see Jesus returning no matter where you are. What Jesus said is that his coming will be very visible to everyone, as visible as the sun coming up and shining around the globe.

Jesus continued:

Matthew 24: 28 For wheresoever the carcase is, there will the eagles be gathered together.

How many times I have stood in the African veld and seen vultures circling. It always means that something has died or been killed. It is obvious. So will the coming of Jesus be. It will be clearly visible.

Matthew 24:29 Immediately after the tribulation of those days shall the sun be darkened, and the moon shall not give her light, and the stars shall fall from heaven, and the powers of the heavens shall be shaken:

Jesus was quoting from a prophecy in Isaiah 13:10: "For the stars of heaven and the constellations thereof shall not give their light: the sun shall be darkened in his going forth, and the moon shall not cause her light to shine." It will be frightening.

Matthew 24:30–31 And then shall appear the sign of the Son of man in heaven: and then shall all the tribes of the earth mourn, and they shall see the Son of man coming in the clouds of heaven with power and great glory. And he shall send his angels with a great sound of a trumpet, and they shall gather together his elect from the four winds, from one end of heaven to the other.

Jesus is not coming back secretly. In Revelation we read, "Behold, he cometh with clouds; and every eye shall see him" (Revelation 1:7), "And the kings of the earth, and the great men, and the rich men, and the chief captains, and the mighty men, and every bondman, and every free man, hid themselves in the dens and in the rocks of the mountains; And said to the mountains and rocks, Fall on us, and hide us from the face of him that sitteth on the throne, and from the wrath of the Lamb: For the great day of his wrath is come; and who shall be able to stand?" (Revelation 6:15–17).

But, for those who really believe the words of Jesus and follow him, he said, "And when these things begin to come to pass, then look up, and lift up your heads; for your redemption draweth nigh" (Luke 21:28). What wonderful news!

Jesus' words are very clear. First, there will come a great tribulation, such as we have never had before. Let us read that verse again:

Matthew 24:21 For then shall be great tribulation, such as was not since the beginning of the world to this time, no, nor ever shall be.

The great tribulation will be followed by the heavenly signs, as we see in the following:

Matthew 24:29 Immediately after the tribulation of those days shall the sun be darkened, and the moon shall not give her light, and the stars shall fall from heaven, and the powers of the heavens shall be shaken:

Only then will Jesus return:

Matthew 24:30 And then shall appear the sign of the Son of man in heaven: and then shall all the tribes of the earth mourn, and they shall see the Son of man coming in the clouds of heaven with power and great glory.

Are we in the great tribulation, a time worse than anything that has ever been before? Not yet! But when it hits us, we will know. Then there will be signs in the heavens, and then Jesus will return.

The prophet Joel was inspired to write:

Joel 2:31 The sun shall be turned into darkness, and the moon into blood, before the great and the terrible day of the Lord come.

It is all very clear: A great tribulation will come. There will be heavenly signs in the sky. Then, Jesus will return! We do not have to speculate. All we need to do is heed the words of Jesus, live by them, and wait. The words of Jesus will unfold. The world will be perplexed and bewildered, but you can look forward with quiet confidence to the coming of the Lord.

Matthew 24:31 And he shall send his angels with a great sound of a trumpet, and they shall gather together his elect from the four winds, from one end of heaven to the other.

A trumpet will sound, and the angels will gather God's elect. This is the same trumpet the apostle Paul wrote about:

1 Thessalonians 4:13–17 But I would not have you to be ignorant, brethren, concerning them which are asleep, that ye sorrow not, even as others which have no hope. For if we believe that Jesus died and rose again, even so them also which sleep in Jesus will God bring with him. For this we say unto you by the word of the Lord, that we which are alive and remain unto the coming of the Lord shall not prevent them which are asleep. For the Lord himself shall descend from heaven with a shout, with the voice of the archangel, and with the trump of God: and the dead in Christ shall rise first: Then we which are alive and remain shall be caught up together with them in the clouds, to meet the Lord in the air: and so shall we ever be with the Lord.

The dead in Christ are resurrected. Why? To meet Christ in the air! Where will Christ be going? Jesus Christ will not be going. He will be coming, he will be returning. Saints have died and have been buried all over the world. They are asleep in their graves, waiting for the return of their Lord, as righteous Job wrote, "O that thou wouldest hide me in the grave, that thou wouldest keep me secret, until thy wrath be past, that thou wouldest appoint me a set time, and remember me! If a man die, shall he live again? all the days of my appointed time will I wait, till my change come. Thou shalt call, and I will answer thee: thou wilt have a desire to the work of thine hands" (Job 14:13–15), and, "For I know that my redeemer liveth, and that he shall stand at the latter day upon the earth: And though after my skin worms destroy this body, yet in [apart from—see note in NIV Study Bible] my flesh shall I see God: whom I shall see for myself, and mine eyes shall behold, and not another; though my reins be consumed within me" (Job 19:25–17).

The resurrection to glorious immortality, at the sounding of the last trumpet, is the future of the saints, as Paul wrote:

> **1 Corinthians 15:51–54** Behold, I shew you a mystery; we shall not all sleep, but we shall all be changed, in a moment, in the twinkling of an eye, at the last trump: for the trumpet shall sound, and the dead shall be raised incorruptible, and we shall be changed. For this corruptible must put on incorruption, and this mortal *must* put on immortality. So when this corruptible shall have put on incorruption, and this mortal shall have put on immortality, then shall be brought to pass the saying that is written, Death is swallowed up in victory.

The glorious resurrection of the saints to immortality is coming. We need to make sure we will be there so that we will be able to say:

> **1 Corinthians 15:55–57** O death, where *is* thy sting? O grave, where *is* thy victory? The sting of death *is* sin; and the strength of sin *is* the law. But thanks *be* to God, which giveth us the victory through our Lord Jesus Christ.

Paul wrote this at a time when Christians were persecuted and killed. Paul had endured incredible hardships, but ahead of them all was the future resurrection of the dead at the time of the return of Jesus Christ. Paul wrote:

1 Corinthians 15:58 Therefore, my beloved brethren, be ye stedfast, unmoveable, always abounding in the work of the Lord, forasmuch as ye know that your labour is not in vain in the Lord.

We can sit around and speculate about when Jesus will return. We can listen to many theories concocted by men, or we can read the words of Jesus, and the words of Paul, and the words of all the holy prophets, and we can look forward to the glorious return of our Savior Jesus Christ to the earth.

Or, we can neglect our salvation; we can fall into the various traps that so many have already fallen into, as Jesus so clearly warned in the rest of his Olivet Prophecy, as we will now see.

The Parable of the Fig Tree

MOST PEOPLE who read Jesus' Olivet Prophecy in Matthew 24 want to stop after they have read about the great tribulation, the heavenly signs, and the return of Jesus. But Jesus was still sitting on the Mount of Olives with his disciples and he continued talking. So we should continue reading. Our Savior is still talking to us, and he is giving us some serious warnings that we need to read and heed. The first warning is in what is called the parable of the fig tree:

> **Matthew 24:32–33** Now learn a parable of the fig tree; when his branch is yet tender, and putteth forth leaves, ye know that summer is nigh: So likewise ye, when ye shall see all these things, know that it is near, even at the doors.

When will we know that the return of Jesus is right at the door? When we see wars, famines, and pestilences? No! When we see people falling away from the church? No! Jesus said, "When you see all these things." What things? The things he had just mentioned: the great tribulation, such as we have never had before, and the heavens shaken. In Luke's account, we read:

Luke 21:25–28 And there shall be signs in the sun, and in the moon, and in the stars; and upon the earth distress of nations, with perplexity; the sea and the waves roaring; Men's hearts failing them for fear, and for looking after those things which are coming on the earth: for the powers of heaven shall be shaken. And then shall they see the Son of man coming in a cloud with power and great glory. And when these things begin to come to pass, then look up, and lift up your heads; for your redemption draweth nigh.

Can there be any doubt that these events have not yet occurred? But they will come, and when they do, those who live to see them will know. There will be no need to guess, no need to speculate about the date of Jesus' return. A preacher friend of mine once said, "We do not need to look at dates. We need to look for figs." That statement is so true. Too many have tried to determine the date of the return of Jesus, a futile exercise. Jesus said we should learn the parable of the fig tree: when it buds, we know summer is near. You do not know the exact date, but you know that it will be very soon. For years I have had fig trees. Other trees would seem to bud early in spring, while the fig tree stayed dormant, without a sign of life. Then, almost overnight, small buds would appear on the fig tree. Summer was on its way. Within a couple of weeks the tree would be covered with leaves. Jesus said, "learn a parable of the fig tree; when his branch is yet tender, and putteth forth leaves, ye know that summer is nigh" (Matthew 24:32).

Has the great tribulation hit us? No. In the 19th century some people saw falling stars over Niagara Falls, and a few other locations. To some it heralded the coming of our Lord, whom they expected in 1844. Then they revised the date to 1845. That was followed by the "great disappointment" because Jesus did not come on a date that those people had tried to calculate using prophecies in the book of Daniel. In the 20th century some also expected Jesus to return. Some looked at 1975 and 1982, and some looked at the end of the millennium. Why were those people mistaken? They also tried to calculate dates using the book of Daniel. They looked at wars, famines pestilence and earthquakes, and saw them as signs of the return of Jesus. They did not really read and believe the exact words of Jesus. Jesus said there will be a great tribulation. Then there will be the heavenly signs. Only then will Jesus return!

Jesus added an important statement:

> **Matthew 24:34** Verily I say unto you, This generation shall not pass, till all these things be fulfilled.

Which generation was Jesus talking about? The generation of the original disciples has long since passed away; so have many more generations. Jesus said that the generation that sees the real end-time events, will not pass away before he returns. Have we seen these end-time events: great tribulation as never before and the heavens shaken? No. We have not even seen the preaching of the gospel of the Kingdom in all nations, and that was mentioned in Matthew 24:14. There is still a lot to happen. Then, for those who still wish to argue about these words, Jesus said:

> **Matthew 24:35** Heaven and earth shall pass away, but my words shall not pass away.

If people believed the words of Jesus, would they really have thought he would have come back in AD 1000 or AD 2000? Can we really say that Jesus may come back tomorrow, or next year? Not if we believe the words of Jesus.

Does that mean we can just sit back and not worry about the return of Jesus? *Not at all!* Where are we now? Jesus told his disciples, "And ye shall hear of wars and rumours of wars: see that ye be not troubled: for all *these things* must come to pass, but the end is not yet" (Matthew 24:6). That is where we still are. Yes, the end is not yet, but we are heading for a time of trouble such as the world has never seen. It will come! I know it may be difficult for those of us who live in our nice homes, drive our nice cars, and eat our good food, to think of a time when all this will be taken away, when we will enter a time of trouble such as never was. But it is going to happen, sooner or later. The generations that saw the horrors of World Wars I and II are now dying. As I am writing this, it has been announced that the last surviving Australian who fought in World War I has just died. There is one American left who fought in that same war. Those who saw six million Jews exterminated in Hitler's concentration camps will not be with us much longer. How many of the new generation remember the Battle of Britain, Dunkirk, Pearl Harbor, and that thirty million people from the Soviet Union died in World War II? Thirty million! Can we imagine that? It happened, and Jesus said we face a future that is going to be far worse than that. Terrifying times will come!

No One Knows the Day or the Hour

IT IS amazing how often Christians have speculated or tried to predict, or calculate, when Jesus would return. Through the ages, groups of Christians have thought that Jesus' return was imminent, only to be greatly disappointed. Preachers are still speculating, trying to predict, and trying to calculate when Jesus will return. What did Jesus say?

Let us continue in the Olivet Prophecy:

Matthew 24:36 But of that day and hour knoweth no *man*, no, not the angels of heaven, but my Father only.

What an amazing statement. Jesus said that the angels did not know when he would return. Jesus said only the Father knew. If only the Father knows, who are we to speculate and try to predict when Jesus will return? How absurd! Even after all the prophetic statements Jesus gave on the Mount of Olives, he still concluded with the words, "But of that day and hour knoweth no *man*." Even those who live into the real end-time events will not know the day and hour of Jesus' return.

In 1963, the minister who baptized me, and who then became a great friend of mine told me, "We do not know the day or the hour, but we can know the year." He was convinced he knew the year of Jesus' return. That year came and went, so did many more. Then the new millennium came. Some time after that my friend died, without seeing the return of Jesus.

Does that mean we should just forget about Jesus' return? *No!* Let us read further:

> **Matthew 24:37–39** But as the days of Noe [Noah] *were*, so shall also the coming of the Son of man be. For as in the days that were before the flood they were eating and drinking, marrying and giving in marriage, until the day that Noe entered into the ark, and knew not until the flood came, and took them all away; so shall also the coming of the Son of man be.

What Jesus is telling us is that it is so easy to carry on our lives as if nothing will happen. "Eat, drink, and be merry," some might say, "why worry? Jesus is not coming tomorrow." How foolish. Jesus may not be coming tomorrow, or next year, or the year after that. But what if you died tonight? Noah preached for years while he was building the ark (Genesis 6). One can only imagine Noah building this big ship, miles from the ocean. Some people would have been intrigued. They would have come to watch and maybe listen to what Noah was saying. After a while, they would have said, "Crazy Noah, all these years, he has been building this ship, miles away from the sea. He says the world is going to be destroyed. He's been saying that for years, but nothing has happened." Then their children, then grandchildren, would have come to look at what Noah was doing. Eventually, they would all have become bored and gone home.

The crowds must have gathered again when the animals entered the ark. What a spectacle. Even the miracle of seeing the animals walk into the ark encouraged no one to follow. Finally, God closed the door of the ark, and the flood came, and, except for the eight members of Noah's family (2 Peter 2:5), no one was saved.

The same can happen to us. How long have preachers talked about the return of Jesus? The apostles talked about it almost two thousand years ago. But Jesus has not come, and from what we can see, he will not come tomorrow. But for you and me, the end could come right now. Why? Because, we could die today, or tomorrow, or the next day! Then what? "For we must all appear before the judgment seat of Christ; that every one may receive the things *done* in *his* body, according to that he hath done, whether *it be* good or bad" (2 Corinthians 5:10). Are we ready to stand before Jesus Christ in the Judgment? Are we ready? Are we really ready? Could you really stand in front of Jesus Christ and say, "Lord, I read your words, I believed them, and I tried to live by them"? Most people have never taken the time to read the words of Jesus. Now is the time for you to take your Bible and start reading the words of Jesus for yourself!

What was it really like in the days of Noah?

> **Genesis 6:5** And God saw that the wickedness of man *was* great in the earth, and *that* every imagination of the thoughts of his heart *was* only evil continually.

Is this where our world is heading? Is wickedness and evil increasing? Jesus also said:

> **Luke 17:26–27** And as it was in the days of Noe, so shall it be also in the days of the Son of man. They did eat,

they drank, they married wives, they were given in marriage, until the day that Noe entered into the ark, and the flood came, and destroyed them all.

Oh, yes, in Noah's day, people ate and drank, married and had children, while wickedness increased all around. We eat and drink, we marry and have children, while everything around us is like an out-of-control, runaway roller coaster heading inexorably downward to destruction.

Jesus added:

Luke 17:28–30 Likewise also as it was in the days of Lot; they did eat, they drank, they bought, they sold, they planted, they builded; but the same day that Lot went out of Sodom it rained fire and brimstone from heaven, and destroyed *them* all. Even thus shall it be in the day when the Son of man is revealed.

We eat, drink, buy, and sell. We plant and build, while our streets are becoming more and more dangerous. The streets of Sodom had become so dangerous that the angels of God had to smite those who wanted to rape them, "with blindness" (Genesis 19:11). Our streets are not like that, some of us may thankfully say, but where are we headed? The apostle Paul wrote, "This know also, that in the last days perilous times shall come. For men shall be lovers of their own selves, covetous, boasters, proud, blasphemers, disobedient to parents, unthankful, unholy, Without natural affection, trucebreakers, false accusers, incontinent, fierce, despisers of those that are good, traitors, heady, highminded, lovers of pleasures more than lovers of God" (2 Timothy 3:1–4). Isn't this what we read in our newspapers? Isn't this what we see on our televisions? Amazingly, Paul added, "Having a form of godliness, but denying the power thereof" (2 Timothy 3:5). Wickedness is increasing all around us, and we convince ourselves that we will be fine because we are good people; we have "a form of godliness."

Jesus continued in the Olivet Prophecy:

> **Matthew 24:40–41** Then shall two be in the field; the one shall be taken, and the other left. Two *women shall be* grinding at the mill; the one shall be taken, and the other left.

Some have used these verses to preach a "secret rapture"—the mistaken idea that Christians are going to be mysteriously whisked away to heaven before all the disasters befall the earth. There will be nothing secret about the coming of Jesus. Through the ages, some have been ready to meet Jesus Christ, but many were not. When Jesus returns, the angels "will gather his elect from the four winds, from one end of the heavens to the other" (Matthew 24:31). That is what Jesus said will happen. The true followers of Jesus Christ, who are still alive on earth at that time, will be taken up to meet the returning Jesus in the air. Yes, one will be taken and another left, but not secretly. We must always be ready.

Jesus continued:

> **Matthew 24:42–44** Watch therefore: for ye know not what hour your Lord doth come. But know this, that if the goodman of the house had known in what watch the thief would come, he would have watched, and would not have suffered his house to be broken up. Therefore be ye also

ready: for in such an hour as ye think not the Son of man cometh.

We do not know when Jesus will return. We also do not know when we are going to die. That is why we must watch and always be ready.

Some like to study the prophecies and try to figure out when Jesus will return. Every indication is that when the events, prior to Christ's coming, begin, they will occur so fast that it will stagger the imagination. "I will wait to repent," may become, "It is too late to repent." That is what happened to the people of Noah's time. *Now* is our time to repent. *Now* is the time to go to God and say, "God be merciful to me a sinner" (Luke 18:13). *Now* is the time to accept Jesus as your Savior. *Now* is the time to heed the words of Jesus, who said, "The time is fulfilled, and the kingdom of God is at hand: repent ye, and believe the gospel" (Mark 1:15). *Now* is the time to start living "by every word that proceedeth out of the mouth of God" (Matthew 4:4), as Jesus said. Jesus could come for you like a thief in the night, when you don't expect him. Jesus may not be coming to this earth today, or tomorrow, or next year, but you could die today, or tomorrow, or the next day. Then you will face Jesus in the Judgment. You must get ready now!

In the New Testament, the apostle Peter knew that Jerusalem was going to be destroyed. Jesus had said so. Peter knew that hundreds of thousands would die, so he warned the people of Jerusalem, "Repent, and be baptized every one of you in the name of Jesus Christ for the remission of sins, and ye shall receive the gift of the Holy [Spirit] (Acts 2:38). He urged the people of his day, "Save yourselves from this untoward generation" (Acts 2:40). Some heeded Peter's warning; three thousand people were baptized

(Acts 2:41) that day. But many did not heed, and when the Roman general, Titus, and his armies came down less than forty years later, some of those who heard Peter speak, along with their children and grandchildren, were killed or taken into slavery.

You too can have your sins forgiven. You too can be ready for Jesus. You too can save yourself from this untoward generation. You do not have to put it off until tomorrow, or next year—or never! You may not have a tomorrow or a next year. What guarantee do you have that you will be here in one, two, or five years? Take a deep breath and hold it. How long could you live if that were your last breath? Not very long! You do not know the day or the hour when Jesus will come, nor do you know the day or hour you will die.

How remarkable that after all that Jesus had said and predicted in his Olivet Prophecy, he still said, "Watch therefore: for ye know not what hour your Lord doth come" (Matthew 24:42). Despite all he said about end-time events, he said we would not know the "day and hour" (Matthew 24:36), and that he would come "in such an hour as ye think not" (Matthew 24:44). That is truly amazing. If Jesus had come in the 1970s, some would have said, "We knew he was going to come." If Jesus had come at the end of the millennium, others would have said, "We knew he was coming." If he came right now, many would say, "We were expecting him." But Jesus said that he would come, "in such an hour as ye think not." Please keep reading the words of Jesus!

My Lord Delayeth His Coming

THROUGH THE ages, Christians have expected Jesus to return, and he didn't. One of the most interesting things to look at is how Christians have acted when Jesus did not return as they expected. Some carried on faithfully following Jesus until they died. Others did not. Let's continue through the Olivet Prophecy and see another serious warning Jesus gave:

> **Matthew 24:45–46** Who then is a faithful and wise servant, whom his lord hath made ruler over his household, to give them meat in due season? Blessed is that servant, whom his lord when he cometh shall find so doing.

Will we continue doing the Lord's work until he comes? Or will we get tired? Will we say, "There is no sign of him coming," and stop working for God? The wise servant will keep on working until Jesus returns or until he or she dies. Jesus said:

> **Matthew 24:47** Verily I say unto you, that he shall make him ruler over all his goods.

Jesus wants us to keep working, even though we do not

know when he will come back. However, he gave another serious warning:

> **Matthew 24:48–49** But and if that evil servant shall say in his heart, My lord delayeth his coming; and shall begin to smite *his* fellowservants, and to eat and drink with the drunken.

Jesus said two things would happen because people thought that he was staying away a long time. The first is that some would begin to smite their fellow servants. How many times has this happened? It happened in Paul's day. It happened throughout the ages. Christians turned on other Christians. Some were persecuted and put to death in the name of Jesus. Churches have split. Some have drawn disciples away after themselves, as the apostle Paul warned some would do: "I know that after I leave, savage wolves will come in among you and will not spare the flock. Even from your own number men will arise and distort the truth in order to draw away disciples after them. So be on your guard! Remember that for three years I never stopped warning each of you night and day with tears" (Acts 20:29–31). Others turned against the followers of Jesus and persecuted and killed them. What a terrible indictment against Christians. Because Jesus had not returned and seemed to be staying away a long time, Christians have turned against each other. To non-Christians, it looks like chaos and confusion. Instead of Christians gathering, they scatter. Jesus said, "He that is not with me is against me; and he that gathereth not with me scattereth abroad" (Matthew 12:30). What a shame! Instead of continuing in the Lord's work, gathering sheep for Jesus, many sheep have been scattered.

The second thing Jesus said would happen is that they would "eat and drink with the drunken" (Matthew 24:49). How many former Christians are now, back in the world, back with their old ways of life, acting as if Jesus will never return? "Let us eat and drink, for tomorrow we die" (1 Corinthians 15:32), they say. That is so true. Sooner or later they will die, and they will face Jesus in the Judgment. Jesus warned:

> **Matthew 24:50–51** The lord of that servant shall come in a day when he looketh not for *him*, and in an hour that he is not aware of, and shall cut him asunder, and appoint *him* his portion with the hypocrites: there shall be weeping and gnashing of teeth.

Jesus will come in an hour in which that wicked servant does not expect him, and "and shall cut him asunder, and appoint *him* his portion with the hypocrites: there shall be weeping and gnashing of teeth." What a serious warning! As we start thinking that Jesus is staying away a long time, we need to be very careful how we act. Will we keep doing the work of God even though Jesus has not returned, or will we turn against the followers of Jesus? Will we start eating and drinking with the drunkards as if there is no tomorrow? If we do, there will be a fearful tomorrow when we have to face the living God, "For we know him that hath said, Vengeance *belongeth* unto me, I will recompense, saith the Lord. And again, The Lord shall judge his people. *It is* a fearful thing to fall into the hands of the living God" (Hebrews 10:30–31).

Yes, Jesus warned, when someone thinks, "My lord delayeth his coming," he may begin "to smite his fellow servants, and to eat and drink with the drunken." This has happened time and again. The apostle John, the disciple "whom Jesus loved" (John 13:23), wrote, "Diotrephes, who loveth to have the preeminence among them, receiveth us not. Wherefore, if I come, I will remember his deeds which he doeth, prating against us with malicious words: and not content therewith, neither doth he himself receive the brethren, and forbiddeth them that would, and casteth *them* out of the church" (3 John 9–10). Jesus had not come back, so some turned against the very disciple whom Jesus loved.

What about us? Now that Jesus has not arrived when we may have expected him, what have we done? Some who used to be so united in love, brothers who used to "dwell together in unity" (Psalm 133:1), while they were eagerly looking forward to the return of Christ, have now turned against each other in viciousness. This is what Jesus said would happen. He warned that some would beat their fellow servants and eat and drink with the drunken. What are *you* doing? More importantly, what *will* you do if Jesus delays his coming even further?

Matthew chapter 24 ends at this point, but chapters and verses were only put in Bibles when they were printed. They were never part of the original manuscripts. Let us continue with the words of Jesus in the Olivet Prophecy, which continue in chapter 25.

The Parable of the Ten Virgins

JESUS' OLIVET Prophecy continues in the next chapter of Matthew. The chapter breaks were inserted many years later; they were not part of the original writing.

Matthew 25:1 Then shall the kingdom of heaven be likened unto ten virgins, which took their lamps, and went forth to meet the bridegroom.

"Then." When is that? The time Jesus was talking about at the end of Matthew 24, the time when there would be faithful servants who would continue working, and unfaithful servants who would turn on the fellow laborers, or who would begin to eat and drink with the drunkards. At that time, these virgins go to meet the bridegroom.

It is always exciting to see people when they first become Christians. They are filled with a "first love" (Revelation 2:4). They want to be with Jesus, and they eagerly look forward to his return. They pray and they study their Bibles. Yes, they are like the ten virgins, lamps in hand, who want to meet the bridegroom.

Now notice:

> **Matthew 25:2–5** And five of them were wise, and five *were* foolish. They that *were* foolish took their lamps, and took no oil with them: But the wise took oil in their vessels with their lamps. While the bridegroom tarried, they all slumbered and slept.

Jesus is continuing with the same theme. He, the bridegroom, "tarried"—he took his time to return. What happened to the ten virgins? They *all* fell asleep! All of them! Some of us may think we are wise, not foolish, Christians, that we would never be foolish and fall asleep. But, it is so easy to fall asleep spiritually, not to be watchful, thinking everything is all right.

> **Matthew 25:6–8** And at midnight there was a cry made, Behold, the bridegroom cometh; go ye out to meet him. Then all those virgins arose, and trimmed their lamps. And the foolish said unto the wise, Give us of your oil; for our lamps are gone out.

The time would come when a cry would ring out, "Behold, the bridegroom cometh; go ye out to meet him." Some would wake up and be ready to respond to the call. Some wouldn't. Jesus said that the foolish virgins did not take enough oil to last the length of time needed. Why is it that so many Christians do not stay the course? They give up. They quit. They become spiritually empty. They go to others looking for help, but they won't get any help there. How often I have seen people proclaim that they were truly Christians, that they knew the truth, that they knew what they believed, and that they looked forward to the return of Jesus with great anticipation. Then Jesus did not return, and so very quickly, these same people have gone off to find spiritual oil somewhere else. But, they won't find it there.

> **Matthew 25:9** But the wise answered, saying, Not so; lest there be not enough for us and you: but go ye rather to them that sell, and buy for yourselves.

How many of us think we can fix things later, we can get ready for God *later*, and we can repent *later*? When will it be *too late*?

> **Matthew 25:10** And while they went to buy, the bridegroom came; and they that were ready went in with him to the marriage: and the door was shut.

The door was shut, just like the door of Noah's ark. It was too late. Those on the outside had time to enter the ark, but they waited and waited. They were too busy "doing their own thing"—like we tend to do, living our lives as if nothing will change, everything will continue as it is.

> **Matthew 25:11–12** Afterward came also the other virgins, saying, Lord, Lord, open to us. But he answered and said, Verily I say unto you, I know you not.

Can you imagine Jesus saying to you, "I know you not"? Of course you can't. It is far too horrible to imagine. It is far easier to think that Jesus will receive you, that you will be ready. But Jesus said some will not be ready, and they will hear those dreadful words,

"I know you not!" Of the two billion Christians on Earth today, is there one who thinks that Jesus will say to him or her, "I know you not"? I doubt it. We all think we are ready. We all think we belong to Jesus. Let's remind ourselves that Jesus also said, "Not every one that saith unto me, Lord, Lord, shall enter into the kingdom of heaven; but he that doeth the will of my Father which is in heaven. Many will say to me in that day, Lord, Lord, have we not prophesied in thy name? and in thy name have cast out devils? and in thy name done many wonderful works? And then will I profess unto them, I never knew you: depart from me, ye that work iniquity" (Matthew 7:21–23). Can we really proclaim that we are working for the Lord, working for Jesus, and still be utterly out of tune with Jesus? That seems so impossible, but those are the words of Jesus Christ of Nazareth! Then, here in the Olivet Prophecy, Jesus repeats his earlier statement:

Matthew 25:13 Watch therefore, for ye know neither the day nor the hour wherein the Son of man cometh.

Notice, in Matthew 24:44, Jesus said, "Therefore be ye also ready: for in such an hour as ye think not the Son of man cometh." Jesus then warned about those evil servants who would turn against their fellow servants. He followed that warning with the parable of the ten virgins who fell asleep. The five foolish virgins lost out; so can we.

In conclusion, Jesus repeated, in Matthew 25:13, "Watch therefore, for ye know neither the day nor the hour wherein the Son of man cometh." It is clear that, through the ages, when some have thought that Jesus "tarried", some would turn against their fellow servants; go back into the world: or would fall asleep spiritually.

Jesus' warning was there for them, and it is there for us. How have we acted, when the return of Jesus seemed to have been delayed? How will we act if the return of Jesus is delayed even longer? Because we do not know the day or the hour, we have to keep watch. We have to always be ready.

The Parable of the Talents

WE SHOULD remind ourselves that the Olivet Prophecy started when the disciples asked Jesus, "Tell us, when shall these things be? and what *shall be* the sign of thy coming, and of the end of the world?" (Matthew 24:3). Matthew chapters 24 and 25 are all the words Jesus spoke in answer to this question. Most of us like to focus on end-time prophecies, rather than on all the teaching Jesus gave to the disciples that day. But we should focus on *all* that Jesus said to his disciples. That way, we will know what we, as Christians, ought to be doing. So let's continue with all the words Jesus spoke to the disciples on the Mount of Olives. He continued:

> **Matthew 25:14–15** For *the kingdom of heaven is* as a man travelling into a far country, *who* called his own servants, and delivered unto them his goods. And unto one he gave five talents, to another two, and to another one; to every man according to his several ability; and straightway took his journey.

This is known as Jesus' parable of the talents. Jesus likened himself to a man who entrusted his property to his servants. To one, he gave five talents, to another two, and to another one talent. The talent was a unit of money. Then he left.

Matthew 25:16–18 Then he that had received the five talents went and traded with the same, and made *them* other five talents. And likewise he that *had received* two, he also gained other two. But he that had received one went and digged in the earth, and hid his lord's money.

The master gave them talents, or money, to use. There would be a time when the Master would come back. We need to remember that there is going to come a time when Jesus will return, and he will want to know what we have done with what we have been given:

Matthew 25:19–23 After a long time the lord of those servants cometh, and reckoneth with them. And so he that had received five talents came and brought other five talents, saying, Lord, thou deliveredst unto me five talents: behold, I have gained beside them five talents more. His lord said unto him, Well done, *thou* good and faithful servant: thou hast been faithful over a few things, I will make thee ruler over many things: enter thou into the joy of thy lord. He also that had received two talents came and said, Lord, thou deliveredst unto me two talents: behold, I have gained two other talents beside them. His lord said unto him, Well done, good and faithful servant; thou hast been faithful over a few things, I will make thee ruler over many things: enter thou into the joy of thy lord.

The master had given the servants talents, a sum of money, according to their abilities. Two servants doubled the money entrusted to them so, with both of them, the master was well pleased. But there was one more servant:

Matthew 25:24–27 Then he which had received the one talent came and said, Lord, I knew thee that thou art an hard man, reaping where thou hast not sown, and gathering where thou hast not strawed: and I was afraid, and went and hid thy talent in the earth: lo, *there* thou hast *that is* thine. His lord answered and said unto him, *Thou* wicked and slothful servant, thou knewest that I reap where I sowed not, and gather where I have not strawed: Thou oughtest therefore to have put my money to the exchangers, and *then* at my coming I should have received mine own with usury.

Some of us think that we have so little to offer to God, we have so little ability, so we do nothing. We bury the one talent God has given us, and we think God will be happy with it. We expect Jesus to return and say to us, "Don't worry, I know you only had a little ability and that you could not do very much. That is all right. I will accept you just as you are. You can enter into my kingdom." That is what we may think Jesus will say. The reality is so different. Jesus called the man who hid his talent and did not use it a "wicked and slothful servant!"

Notice Jesus' next words:

Matthew 25:28–30 Take therefore the talent from him, and give *it* unto him which hath ten talents. For unto every one that hath shall be given, and he shall have abundance: but from him that hath not shall be taken away even that which he hath. And cast ye the unprofitable servant into outer darkness: there shall be weeping and gnashing of teeth.

So much of what Jesus said is so different from what we may imagine. Not only will Jesus have that wicked, slothful servant thrown into outer darkness, Jesus will take his talent and give it to the man who had the most, the man with the ten talents. Why would Jesus do that? Why give it to the man who had the most? Because that man would produce the most with it!

This is Jesus talking about the end-time, the time of his return, and he says we must produce. We cannot sit around and do nothing. We cannot expect Jesus to receive us with our nothingness. We must produce. How different that is from most Christian messages. Most Christian messages say, "You don't have to do anything. Jesus did it all for you. Come just as you are." Jesus said the man who does not produce, who does not work and increase, will be thrown into outer darkness, and there will be weeping and gnashing of teeth.

Yes, Christians need to be busy; they need to be doing something. "But what?" you may ask. Let's continue reading the words of Jesus:

> **Matthew 25:31–40** When the Son of man shall come in his glory, and all the holy angels with him, then shall he sit upon the throne of his glory: and before him shall be gathered all nations: and he shall separate them one from another, as a shepherd divideth *his* sheep from the goats: and he shall set the sheep on his right hand, but the goats on the left. Then shall the King say unto them on his right hand, Come, ye blessed of my Father, inherit the kingdom prepared for you from the foundation of the world: For I was an hungred, and ye gave me meat: I was thirsty, and ye gave me drink: I was a stranger, and ye took me in: naked, and ye clothed me: I was sick, and ye visited me: I was in prison, and ye came unto me. Then shall the righteous answer him, saying, Lord,

when saw we thee an hungred, and fed *thee*? or thirsty, and gave *thee* drink? When saw we thee a stranger, and took *thee* in? or naked, and clothed *thee*? Or when saw we thee sick, or in prison, and came unto thee? And the King shall answer and say unto them, Verily I say unto you, Inasmuch as ye have done *it* unto one of the least of these my brethren, ye have done *it* unto me.

What should we be doing while we wait for Jesus to return? Jesus tells us clearly. We should feed the hungry, give water to the thirsty, look after strangers, clothe those who need to be clothed, visit those who are sick or in prison. This, Jesus said, is what we ought to do, and if we do it, Jesus will consider it as if we did it for Jesus himself.

But what about those who do nothing:

Matthew 25:41–45 Then shall he say also unto them on the left hand, Depart from me, ye cursed, into everlasting fire, prepared for the devil and his angels: For I was an hungred, and ye gave me no meat: I was thirsty, and ye gave me no drink: I was a stranger, and ye took me not in: naked, and ye clothed me not: sick, and in prison, and ye visited me not. Then shall they also answer him, saying, Lord, when saw we thee an hungred, or athirst, or a stranger, or naked, or sick, or in prison, and did not minister unto thee? Then shall he answer them, saying, Verily I say unto you, Inasmuch as ye did *it* not to one of the least of these, ye did *it* not to me.

Jesus is not on Earth today; he has not yet returned. But all around us are the brothers and sisters of Jesus. They need help, they need to be fed, clothed, and visited. We can sit around and speculate about when Jesus will return, or we can stay busy with the Lord's work. That is our choice. It is a serious choice. How many of us are concerned about wars, famines, pestilence, and earthquakes as signs of the return of Jesus? Meanwhile, all around us, there are people who need to be helped. The gospel needs to be preached, and what do we do? Some bury their talent, thinking Jesus will be happy with it. Or, we close our eyes to the suffering around us. Would Jesus do that? Do we forget that when Jesus returns, he will reward us according to what we have done? Notice the last words of Jesus' Olivet Prophecy:

> **Matthew 25:46** And these shall go away into everlasting punishment: but the righteous into life eternal.

The one thing we should never forget is that when Jesus returns, he will reward us according to what we have done with what he has given us. The reward for some will be to rule with Christ in the kingdom of God. For others, unfortunately, it will be eternal punishment, which will be death in the "lake of fire" (Revelation 20:15).

So Jesus ended his words to the disciples on the Mount of Olives. "And it came to pass, when Jesus had finished all these sayings, he said unto his disciples, Ye know that after two days is *the feast of* the passover, and the Son of man is betrayed to be crucified" (Matthew 26:1–2). Jesus and the disciples then walked down the Mount of Olives. Below them lay Jerusalem, the "city of peace," but it would see very little peace in the next two thousand years. Instead, it saw wars and more wars. It still faces war. The end has not yet come.

What Have We Learned?

WE HAVE learned that no one knows when Jesus will return. Through the centuries, people thought Jesus would return in their day, but he did not. The end of the second millennium came. Millions celebrated the dawn of the new millennium. Some thought Jesus would return at that time, but he did not.

Jesus warns us of false teachings about his coming. He said, "Take heed that ye be not deceived: for many shall come in my name, saying, I am *Christ*; and the time draweth near: go ye not therefore after them" (Luke 21:8). If someone tells us, "The time is near," we should not follow him or her. The way to avoid any false teaching is to stick to what Jesus said.

Our world has seen wars, famines, pestilences, and earthquakes, and it will see many, many more. These are not the signs of the end. That is what Jesus said. When Jesus comes, it will be the most spectacular event in all of history. No one will miss it; however, not everyone will be ready for it.

Some, because they thought Jesus was staying away a long time, smote their fellow servants, or will smite their fellow servants. The history of Christianity shows this over and over again. Christians have persecuted and even killed other Christians. What a tragedy. Others have gone back into the world to eat and drink with drunkards. At one time or another, everyone has fallen asleep. When some woke up, they were ready; others were not.

What if Jesus does not return soon? Jesus urged Christians to pray, "Thy kingdom come" (Matthew 6:10). The Kingdom of God will put an end to the suffering of humankind. It will bring peace on Earth. But, for you, Jesus could come tomorrow, or the next day, or next year, because you could die! Will you be ready? May God help you to be ready! In the meantime, we need to be busy. We need to work and produce, not bury the talent Jesus has given us. There is so much to do. Are we preaching the good news that Jesus Christ is our Savior and that he will be returning to set up a Kingdom on this earth that will never end? Are we praying for, and supporting, those who are preaching the good news of the kingdom of God to this dying world?

Conclusion

Why has Jesus not returned? Here are the reasons:

1. Only God the Father knows when he will send Jesus back to this earth. We do not know the day or the hour of Jesus' return, and we cannot calculate it.

2. The gospel of the Kingdom has not been preached to the world as a witness to all nations (Matthew 24:14). There are still far too many people who have no idea what the gospel of the kingdom is. That is what we should be busy doing. Let us continue to do that and help and pray for those who are doing it, and will be doing it.

3. Unbelievable distress, a great tribulation, will come upon the earth before Jesus returns.

4. God is giving humankind time to repent. As the apostle Peter wrote, "The Lord is not slack concerning his promise, as some men count slackness; but is longsuffering to us-ward, not willing that any should perish, but that all should come to repentance" (2 Peter 3:9). You could die at any time. Jesus says to you, "Watch therefore: for ye know not what hour your Lord doth come" (Matthew 24:42).

5. Unfortunately, despite all that Jesus said, some will still spend their time and energy trying to figure out when he will return. After all the mistakes many have made in the past with their calculations, about when Jesus will return, some are still trying to calculate it. A week does not seem to go by without me hearing some new theory about when Jesus will return. Are we never going to believe what Jesus said?

6. There is still so much to do. Most people on Earth are oblivious to the truth of the gospel. The Bible is a closed book to them. Our world is like Isaiah prophesied, "The way of peace they know not; and *there is* no judgment in their goings: they have made them crooked paths: whosoever goeth therein shall not know peace. Therefore is judgment far from us, neither doth justice overtake us: we wait for light, but behold obscurity; for brightness, *but* we walk in darkness. We grope for the wall like the blind, and we grope as if *we had* no eyes: we stumble at noon day as in the night; *we are* in desolate places as dead *men*. We roar all like bears, and mourn sore like doves: we look for judgment, but *there is* none; for salvation, *but* it is far off from us" (Isaiah 59:8–11). But salvation is not far from us. Jesus came to this earth to die as our Savior, and he is going to come back to save the world!

7. The return of Jesus will come in God's good time, but for us, the time to be ready is now. Now is the time to learn what Jesus said, now is the time to live according to the words of Jesus Christ!

If this book has been an inspiration and a blessing to you, please read the follow-up book: *What Is Going To Happen When Jesus Returns?* It may be one of the most exciting books you will ever read.

Epilogue

As I wrote at the beginning of this book, I have waited for the return of Jesus for a very long time. I first thought about it in 1955, when I was a teenager and heard sermons about the coming of our Lord. Like many, through the years, I also looked at possible dates, fully knowing that those dates were just that, speculations that, in the end, would not prove significant. Some dates in prophecy, and history, are significant, of course, but the one date we do not know, and will not know, is when Jesus will return.

All this raises a serious concern. My generation, the one born during World War II, is now starting to die. I myself almost died of a heart attack in 2002. Those of the new generation experienced little of what happened in the twentieth century. They have little comprehension of the events of World War I (1914–18). Most have not even heard the details of the great flu epidemic of 1918 that killed ten times as many Americans as died in the Great War; a flu that, for some reason, was more deadly for people between the ages of twenty and forty than for the usual children and elderly; a flu that, in some towns, killed every single person, the bodies undiscovered until weeks later. So many people died in such a short span of time that the bodies were stacked in piles and covered with saltpeter—potassium nitrate—to preserve them till they could be buried.

This new generation knows little of World War II, of how the virtually unknown Austrian Adolf Hitler came to power in Germany in 1933 and by 1940 had conquered most of Europe and was threatening the rest of the world. It knows little of how Germany and Japan tried to divide the world between themselves and of the massive effort it took, along with many miraculous events, to rid the earth of that scourge. Elderly Jews try desperately to remind this new generation of the Holocaust, the systematic killing of six million Jews in Hitler's death camps. Most in this generation do not know of the war that occurred in Korea, and even the Vietnam War is rather vague in their minds.

This new generation, in so many respects, is profoundly blessed. In the developed world, to have a home, a car, and food in the refrigerator is considered simply normal. Those of this new generation are oblivious to many of the events of the past. I fear for them. True, the generations before mine feared for those in my generation. They knew we would live into fearful times, and we did. My generation was the first to see how humankind could blow itself off the face of the earth in a nuclear conflagration. No wonder we thought the "end times" had arrived. It seems surreal now that, when we were children, we were taught what to do if a nuclear blast were to occur, until we realized that it would be futile, that in the event of a nuclear attack we would all simply be obliterated.

Nuclear bombs still exist. Huge rockets still stand in silos underground, ready to be launched at a moment's notice. Submarines equipped with nuclear weapons still prowl our oceans in a macabre game of hide and seek. Other nations have joined the nuclear club, and some of them are far less stable than the early members, the United States, Britain, France, Russia, and China. Nuclear terrorism has now become a serious threat.

Epilogue

But, in my mind, nothing is more of a threat to the next generation than to repeat history. The history of World War I, despite the desperate warnings of many visionaries like Winston Churchill, was repeated by the grotesque events of World War II. Now those events are fading from our consciousness. The last thing our world would expect is another war in Europe, yet if we look back over the past two millennia, the main focus of our world was always Europe. For almost fifteen-hundred years, our world was divided between a Christian Europe in the north and the Muslim south. Whether we like it or not, the United States of America has, over the past century, been the only power that could step into the fray to prevent Europe from destroying all of civilization. What is going to happen when the United States, for whatever reason, stops exercising that power? Many feel that it was an enormous mistake for United States to get embroiled in the present war in Iraq, and within the past two years there has been a dramatic change in the feeling of the American people about that war. They want that war to end; they want American troops out. If, or when, that happens, the world may end up with another isolationist America, like the one prior to World War II, an America that was not arming itself for war; that was not prepared for the attack on Pearl Harbor; that took two years, from the end of 1941 to 1943, to get its mammoth industrial production capacity geared up for the massive effort needed to finally defeat Germany and Japan in 1945. How many, today, know that Russia fought Germany with American-made weapons? America is no longer the industrial production powerhouse of the world. That production has moved to Asia. Could America today produce what it did by the end of World War II, when it launched a battleship a day?

The age-old division of the world between Christian Europe

and the Muslim south still exists, and for the final climactic end-time events to occur, Europe will have to arm itself. Will America withdraw its power from the world scene, causing a void into which Europe, of necessity, will have to step in to fill? The greatest tragedies of the twentieth century were caused when Germany armed itself. Now Germany does not stand alone. It has become part of a political entity called the European Union. But Europe still faces the same age-old threats: a threat from the southern Muslim peoples, who for centuries attacked Europe, and a threat from the east. Few remember that Hitler's capital was finally overrun by Asiatic hordes that plunged into Berlin from the east.

Out of necessity Europe will have to arm itself against future threats. But for those of us who recall the events of the past century, the thought of a Christian world arming itself should fill us with horror and grim foreboding of what the ultimate outcome of that will be: another world conflagration starting in Europe and drawing all nations into a vortex of violence that will make the words of Jesus truly meaningful, "And except those days should be shortened, there should no flesh be saved [alive—Moffatt translation]" (Matthew 24:22). That is the world my children and their children will live into. I pray that I will not see it.

It has been too easy for those of my generation to speculate about the return of Christ, as we lived in a world of relative peace and in nations that were blessed with so much. Now our children have inherited that world, a world of abundance—if we close our eyes to the wars, famines, disease, natural disasters, and pestilence that many peoples still face on a daily basis. The greatest danger the next generation faces is that it might be oblivious to the events of the past and therefore destined to repeat them. Some things have not changed over the past few years: our continents are still the same; we still find the same nations living in the same countries they lived in; and they still face the same threats. One thing, however, has changed: technology. Hitler spent just six years from the time he came to power till he launched his first offensive. Then, after a pause, his armies ran over western Europe in a few weeks. That was at a time when no aircraft had broken the sound barrier, when no rocket had been launched to bring devastation on an enemy, and tanks could barely go twenty miles an hour, and yet, Hitler's warfare was called *blitzkrieg*—lightning war. What will a future war, fought at speeds, higher than the speed of sound, be like?

The greatest danger future generations face is that they live too far from the past, a past that could warn them about the future. World War II did not come as a surprise to many who had lived through World War I, but World War III, undoubtedly, will come as a fearful surprise to a generation that knows nothing about world wars.

Do I believe that I will see the return of Jesus in my lifetime? I doubt that seriously, more so as I have stood at death's door on several occasions. For me to hear preachers say, "Jesus will come soon," or "It is just around the corner," or "It is going to happen within the next ten or twenty years," is just foolish talking, and it is not truly based on scripture. One thing is absolutely certain: the words of Jesus Christ are just as true today as they have been through the centuries. They have always encouraged the people of God to continue to do what is right and to continue to do a work for God, no matter what the circumstances in the world may be. The fact that Jesus Christ will return as King of kings and Lord of lords (Revelation 19:16) is absolutely certain. Please read my forthcoming book, *Understanding the Book of Revelation*. The book of Revelation clearly spells out the events that still have to occur on this earth of ours before the great and glorious return of our Savior and our King—Jesus Christ!

Other books by Daniel Botha

What Is Going To Happen When Jesus Returns?

Have you ever heard a sermon that told you exactly what it is going to be like when Jesus returns? There are so many prophecies in the Bible that tell us about the return of Jesus, and what he will do when he gets back, but so few turn to those scriptures. Instead, the return of Jesus is vague in most people's minds. What will his return be like? What will happen when he returns? What will happen after he returns? The return of Jesus is going to be the most frightening event that this world will ever witness, but it is also going to be the most glorious. *What Is Going To Happen When Jesus Returns?* is a step-by-step explanation of the events that will happen when Jesus returns.

Understanding the Book of Revelation

At the end of the New Testament we find a book that is generally entitled: The Revelation of St. John the divine. But the book starts with the words, "The Revelation of Jesus Christ, which God gave unto him, to shew unto his servants things which must shortly come to pass; and he sent and signified *it* by his angel unto his servant John" (Revelation 1:1). It is not the revelation of John, it is the revelation of Jesus Christ, and it was given to show his servants, "things which must shortly come to pass." Through the ages, the Book of Revelation showed the servants of God what was about to happen to them. It was a guiding light to them through the centuries. It was not just an "end-time" book. It has always been a book *of revelation*, a book of revealing, yet to most people it seems like the most obscure book ever written. It does not need to be. *Understanding the Book of Revelation* is a step-by-step journey through the fascinating, and understandable, Book of Revelation.